BACK TO BASICS WITH THE 'SAKE' PHILOSOPHY

AM I CHEF?

GEORGE E. HILL
copyright 2014

First Published 2014, Melbourne, Australia.
2nd Reprint May 2014, Melbourne, Australia.
3rd Reprint February 2016, Melbourne, Australia.

Published by RW Marketing Pty Ltd
Layout, design and cover design by RW Marketing Pty Ltd
Cover Photography by Patrick Varney Photography

ISBN 978-0-646-91852-5

Reproduction and Communication for educational purposes
The Australian Copyright Act 1968 (The Act) permits a maximum of one chapter or 10% of the pages of this work, whichever is the greater, to be reproduced and/or communicated by any educational institute for its educational purposes, provided that the educational institute (or the body that administers it) has given remuneration notice to Copyright Agency Limited (CAL) under the Act.

Reproduction and Communication for other purposes
All rights reserved. Except as permitted under the Act (for example, any fair dealing for the purposes of study, research, criticism or review) no part of this book may be reproduced, stored in a retrieval system, or transmitted in any form or by any means, electronic, mechanical, photocopying, recording, or otherwise, without prior written permission.

Am I Chef? © George E. Hill 2014

All inquiries should be made to the author:
george@salonculinaire.com

CONTENTS

ACKNOWLEDGMENT
DEDICATION
FORWARD
THE AUTHOR

introduction 2
history - my introduction into a commercial kitchen 6

ATTRIBUTES
for goodness SAKE, are we cooks or are we chefs?... 16
the sake philosophy - who is a chef?... 26
skills - physical and conceptual ability 30
attitude - characteristics and personality traits 34
knowledge - essential theory and practical ability 38
experience - obligatory commercial participation 58
titles - culinary titles and ranks 68

ISSUES
for goodness' sake, self-inflicted issues.. 84
training - for's and againts formal and non formal training 86
associations - how professional is professional 92
competitions - it is time to remove the mystery.. 96
uniform - do chefs understand branding?... 102
bully beef - is being a bully, a chef's natural temperament? 108
media - when it comes to tv, everybody's tastes are different 112
spelling - should that windyloo be vindaloo? 116
allergies - who is responsible, the chef or the client? 122
menu planning - are young guns losing passion?.. 126

CUSTOMS
food presentation - it is a question of era 130
ettiquette - culinary customs and traditions.. 140
professional codes - australian culinary codes of practice.................................. 148
professional codes - australian culinary codes of practice.................................. 150
appendix 1 - chef's speak 156
appendix 2 - common culinary technical terms & cookery descriptions 160
hot off the press
- penalty Rates, are they an industry problem or a political issue?..................... 170
- contradictions; Are they showing a dying profession?.................................... 174

acknowledgment

When Richard and I initially discussed the idea of utilising the vast skills behind the RW team to publish and promote this book, I immediately became conscious that this was more than an ideal partnership.

"AM I CHEF" is all about standards, as is RW Marketing, "AM I CHEF" focuses on chefs who practice in the hospitality Industry as does RW Marketing, and "AM I CHEF" has a commitment to excellence and achieving positive outcomes, as does RW demonstrate in all of its Tourism and Hospitality Industry projects, evidenced by the results the company consistently achieves.

I have had the pleasure of being associated with many Australian, Hospitality and Tourism industry's brightest minds in media and have done so over forty years. Experiencing the industry mature from the early days in a unsophisticated market to the contemporary complex market where Australia must keep up with other global leaders and Richard Warneke who leads the RW team would rank among the very best mentalities I've ever encountered.

It takes the likes of the RW team who have the passion to be understanding, innovative and creative to deliver a fresh angle in an ever growing diverse media publishing, technology and telecommunications driven market, where success on the process of constantly redesigning and leading from the front.

I am delighted that Richard and his team are involved in redesigning and promoting this book.

George Hill.

dedication

I particularly wish to thank my patient wife, Catherine, and dear friend Norma Seip, for reading draft scripts and providing valuable input into its final form and grateful for the invaluable input from many industry colleagues.

I also acknowledge how fortunate I have been in my career to be associated with great mentors who shaped my own thoughts, and who have assisted me on the path towards developing the 'SAKE' Philosophy.

The concepts in here are not new or magically created. They represent views that I formed from the many fine chefs and friends met along a road where destiny determined that I would enjoy a career that was in fact a hobby.

To work every day, doing what one loves and then be paid is such a rarity. Why me? I will never know.

forward

"AM I CHEF?" is a very interesting book that encourages readers to consider the future of a career as a chef.

George explains the fundamentals that comprise a commercial chef He defines their skills, attitude, knowledge and experience, describes cookery industry titles and explores many issues that face an ever-changing world. The book concludes with chapters on culinary slang, codes of practice and basic global culinary terminology.

George knows his stuff and this book challenges and advances culinary history, an aspect of commercial cookery that we are both engaged in.

At times, **"AM I CHEF?"** is controversial, yet it illustrates innovation and passion, which is an ingrained characteristic in a chef. Its terminology and definitions really capture the true attitude and essence of, *"Am I a cook or chef"? Have chef's titles been hijacked? Are chef's innovative or creative?* In addition, many other intriguing issues are explored.

"I encourage you be the judge of those!"   *John Mc Fadden*

> *John Mc Fadden is a highly respected Australian Executive Chef who has evolved from an award winning career in fine dining, restaurants, cafes, hotels and catering companies; first and business class lounges and boarding schools and culminating as Executive chef of 24 major properties across Sydney. John is the senior professional cookery judge who chairs the annual "Chef of the Year" competitions across Australia*

the author

George Hill is one of six living Australian Culinary Federation (Victoria) Black Hat Chefs in Australia and is a designated Pioneer amongst Les Toques Blanches Executive Chefs of Australia.

His industry experiences include being an apprentice cook, chef de partie, sous chef, chef de cuisine, executive chef, commercial cookery teacher, commercial cookery educational manager, hospitality consultant, and small business owner-operator.

In 1957, he commenced his career as an apprentice cook in the Cumberland Hotel London. In 1966, he immigrated to Australia and became an Australian citizen in 1979. His first job in Australia was as a chef at the Royal Automobile Club of Victoria in Melbourne. In 1971, he became a commercial cookery teacher at the William Angliss Institute of TAFE in Melbourne where he eventually led a teaching staff of more than 30 in the 'Foods department'. Hill was subsequently promoted to one of the four program managers of the institute.

He won gold for Australia in the 1980 Culinary Olympics; judged in the International World Skills in 1983 and during that year received the Australian Foodservice Manufacturers Association Award. In 1988 he was awarded a Churchill Fellowship; received a National Award of Excellence from the National Association of Food service Equipment Suppliers in 1994 and honoured with a National Award of Excellence from the Foodservice Suppliers Association Australia in 2010.

In 1986, Hill moved to the new Hospitality Facility at Chisholm Institute in Victoria to head the Tourism and Hospitality Faculty for eight years.

In 2000, Hill was bestowed the Sidney Taylor Memorial Black Hat Award. This honour is considered by chefs in Australia to be the highest industry achievement possible.

After leaving education he owned and operated the externally rated five-star and multiple awarded 'Rosehill Lodge'. Hill co-authored the only technical book on the topic of margarine and butter sculpture; was director of the World Championships in Commercial Cookery in Melbourne and judged internationally in Austria, New Zealand and Fiji.

In 2008, Hill initiated the 'Australian Culinary Code of Practices' for professional cooks and chefs that has been subsequently adopted by every professional chefs' association in Australia.

Nothing ever achieved is the effort of one person.

01. introduction

introduction

Using a pun, "For goodness sake, that says it all" The SAKE philosophy (pronounced as in HAKE or RAKE representing **S**kills, **A**ttitude, **K**nowledge, and **E**xperience) was written to respond to a number of issues facing commercial cookery.

Over recent times, I became aware that among many increasing demands on the cookery industry, there are financial and political pressures placed on institutes to dilute curriculum that has the potential to de-skill commercial cookery.

While recently judging young guns in hot competitions, I was appalled at the lack of straightforward technical skills, the knowing of simple culinary terminology, and the lack of many other facets that should be found in a chef; typical skills and basic knowledge that were habitual not so long ago. Seeing the way many attempted to prepare a béchamel, fillet a fish, cut a chicken for sauté, make an omelette, or dice an onion frightened me.

Noticing apprentice cooks sitting on the ground in school corridors, their deteriorating dress standards, and their lack of discipline; behaviours sadly disregarded by teaching staff and rationalised as the "Y generation". Additionally the self-inflicted problems by modern guns, who are aided and abetted by the infiltration of many who purposely exploit the title chef and are either unaware or do not care about commercial cookery as a career, made me conclude that someone should identify and record a benchmark based on the past.

While **SAKE** is a philosophy of mine, it only identifies, clarifies, packages and records experiences from the past. It is broad and not necessarily inclusive, however as comprehensive as possible.

I attempt to identify some of the more important issues in commercial cookery, particularly the slide in standards and I sincerely hope all of this is overstated.

If my conclusions are in any small part correct, this slide needs halting, as potentially this could result in destroying a noble occupation.

| introduction

While the top end of the market or fine-dining sector is to be admired for maintaining world-class standards in cuisine, it is primarily the larger middle market and family dining sector that is showing the concerns of declining standards in food service. Chef de cuisines at the finer food services are bitterly complaining that it is extremely difficult to find qualified passionate cooks and chefs, while in family dining, suburban and remote areas, almost impossible.

The **'SAKE'** philosophy identifies in simplest of terms, a benchmark of a chef, while additionally exploring topics that currently are hot for all to debate. After all, sometimes it is just as good to return to the past to repeat the obvious and learn lessons which may forecast the future.

If something has been missed I apologise. Except while attempting to describe what constitutes a chef in simplistic terms, nothing in **'SAKE'** is dramatically new. This is not an attempt to reinvent the wheel. **SAKE** is simply a record for destiny to do what it will.

Why; "Am I Chef"? and not "Am I a Chef"?

02. history

my introduction into a commercial kitchen

My culinary philosophy was set in motion at a very young age. I believe I am a cook; a passion that fired when I was very young, but honoured that some colleagues call me a **CHEF**.

As a young 15 year old entering the workforce it was a little confusing, if not frightening, to enter a commercial kitchen. Was this not my dream come true, having made up my mind to become a cook, about nine years old?

At the age of nearly 15, I thought I was "street wise" gained from my experience of being a paperboy to earn extra cash. The prospect of entering the kitchen on my first full-time job should not have been that frightening and yet why did my confidence appear to slump lower and lower the nearer I got to the kitchen?

In August 1957, on my first day in a commercial kitchen, I started the first day of the rest of my life. The hotel kitchen, in the basement, was large, with stoves, steamers, workbenches, wall fridges and grills on one side separating a long corridor by an extensive gleaming race, no natural light and with heavy steamy air.

I distinctly remember entering the kitchen, full of anxiety about the future, a feeling that I was walking towards my gallows, moreover wearing an oversized cook's coat, a floppy white hat and a necktie that seemed impossible to tie neatly around my neck. As I entered the kitchen I had to nervously walk past a small office with windows positioned so whoever was in there had full view of the kitchen including, on the other side of the corridor, a long line of walk-in fridges.

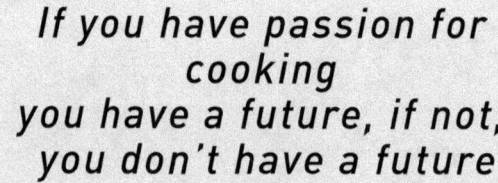

If you have passion for cooking you have a future, if not, you don't have a future

history - my introduction into a commercial kitchen

It was then I heard my very first terrifying words, "Eh boy, Fermez la porte, s'il vous plait". Not understanding French added apprehension to my entrance. In a panic, I desperately tried to straighten my necktie, believing this to be the obvious command which emitted from a short impeccably dressed chef in full white cook's uniform and tall white hat; only to see him burst out laughing as he said in English with a French accent "Boy, I said close the fridge door".

There stood Chef "Devari'e" chief and god of a brigade of 52 cooks not including the 17 apprentices; a little man with a tall white hat, a small but friendly face and deep eyes that you just knew would see everything.

A paradox of a man, both loved and yet feared by his team, who was an inspiring leader of a hot tempered multicultural brigade. The brigade was not multicultural as we understand the word today, but still a gathering of many different nationalities: French sous chefs, Polish, German, Egyptian, Dutch, Swiss and English chef de parties to name a few, all with a fundamental dislike of any other nationality other than their own.

There were several sous chefs in Devari'es brigade and each in turn had several chefs de parties working under them and each partie with their own team of commis, trainee managers, porters, and apprentices. Yet I remember the second most powerful man in the kitchen was the "Aboyeur" or the order caller, who even made the sous chefs jump when he barked. Why so much power I will never know.

I soon learnt that a commercial kitchen is a very structured environment and being both an apprentice and particularly the new baby on the block, meant that I was at the very bottom of the ladder.

My first assignment, for three months, was to work in the mise - en - place ("prep kitchen") on a floor below the main silver service grill.

This was where you served your indenture in order to become an apprentice worthy of working in the main kitchen. This prep kitchen alone was much larger than most large hotel kitchens today and was the busy supply department and core of the many other kitchens in the Cumberland Hotel London.

Every delivery of fresh produce, whether game, poultry, vegetables or fish, came into this prep kitchen first, for initial processing. Whole fish were cleaned and scaled and the chooks and grouse eviscerated and plucked, oyster shells crushed, and vegetables washed. What seemed like a never-ending procession of goods requisitioned out on numerous trolleys that came in empty and left like clockwork on trains out of a major city station as they chuffed to the other areas of the hotel for a further preparation.

Chickens had to be literally drawn and defeathered by their hundreds, fish gutted and filleted, vegetables washed, sorted and counted by the ton, and much more. For ten hours a day, for six days a week, I stood with hands red and sore, feet and back aching and unable to dare to answer back.

However, at last I had survived the ordeal and it was to be my first day in the real world, transferred to the "Silver Grill

Kitchen" (which today, if it still existed, would be the fine dining kitchen). It appeared that I had served my induction and now was to be "promoted" as an apprentice in the Garde Manger, but more importantly, not the baby on the block any more.

The Chef de partie Garde Manger "Chef Castle" not even remembering his first name, as one would only dare to call him by the title "Chef". In this small world of the larder section, there was a smaller god, Chef Castle, who by now must be in the great white kitchen in the sky. He was assisted by one third commis de cuisine, one second commis de cuisine, one trainee manager and two apprentices. I was again at the mercy of the whole team. I was now to be the one who washes, runs and jumps even more than the others.

history - my introduction into a commercial kitchen

We made dressings and mayonnaise, salads, and cold platters. I even remember the rule to break each egg and smell it before separating the yolk from white. I pounded lobster shells, kept the trout alive in large fish tanks. These fish were eventually to be sent to god when the fish partie called for one to be extracted, gutted and cleaned for "Truite au bleu". I often wondered if a wily trout ever survived the deadly ordeal by knowing when one's time was up and swimming to the bottom or hiding in such a way as not to be the one caught this time. Maybe for years an "old man trout" swam around the tank until luck or age caught up.

It was here that I watched in wonder as the chef prepared a Chaud - froid picture from blanched vegetable on a velvet white background and the 20 or more hors d'oeuvre platters made daily for the dining room trolley. **No-one told you, showed you, or gave you handouts; you learnt by sight, taste and smell and became proficient by doing a task over and over; and over again and getting better and faster every time.**

Now after four months and learning to survive, I was next assigned to the roast partie. This partie was not such a large section as the larder with only three of us: the Chef, the 3rd commis and lowly me with mountains of chickens to roast, grouse, and pheasant to truss and now ten hours of standing in front of an oven, soaked in sweat, which was to be my first experience of real heat.

I remember once the chef de partie, in a German accent, dared to tell the Aboyeur that the chicken was off the menu - only to be screamed at by the Aboyeur and Sous chef that he had better get some more on the way and that GREAT KITCHENS WILL ALWAYS HONOUR WHAT THEY HAD ON THE MENU.

At the same time I was immediately dispatched to literally run to another kitchen to obtain a chicken and ordered to be back in minutes or my guts were garters. I soon discovered that the Polish hated the Germans, who hated the English, who hated the French and all considered the Hungarians as fools and took every opportunity to scream abuse to each other to let everyone know when someone stuffed up.

It was here that I learnt that real kitchens made their own convenience foods, only we called it names like "Glace de Viande", prepared from hours of reduction of the roast juices and stock made into a thick, black, meaty molasses and why the other chefs revered this product.

The gods looked down on me and showed mercy and I was to get away from the daily hell of roasting in both the oven and words after only two months in that hell.

My next assignment was to be sent to the soup partie. Here gallons of consommé and other soups were prepared each day from it seemed masses of bones and mirepoix. The soups were made in pots big enough to have a bath; prepared not only for the silver grill dining room, but all the soups required for the banquet kitchen and the many other food outlets of the hotel.

A nice friendly Hungarian chef de partie with whom I worked was probably my best time as an apprentice, as we actually got on together and only two of us would cover the seven days on split shifts. Funnily, none of the other chefs de parties, or apprentices, liked the small, bald-headed man who profusely swore in Hungarian who wore glasses that steamed up as he paddled through the various velouté each day. Still, as far as I was concerned, I was now being treated like a human at last. I actually was given a break now and again to go to the staff kitchen for a meal, for you would not dare eat in the kitchen.

At least not while the chef or Sous chefs were around, needless to say, a sneaky snack sometimes in the afternoon on the rare straight shift. In the staff kitchen, they called it a meal, made from the best of the worst scraps, prepared by cooks that could not cook anywhere else in the industry.

I remember one day, the word got around that the young new French Sous chef (all the Sous chefs were French) was not happy with the apprentices' performances and was planning to move them all as this trivial roster was not done by the head chef, but allocated to one of his minions.

history - my introduction into a commercial kitchen

Ah, this was my first lesson and opportunity to be involved in politics. I was now in the job more than a year and had learnt the lesson that real politics is more doing what you are told by the ones who make the actual decisions than being able to influence someone with more power than you.

There I was at last in the golden partie, "the sauce". A great partie and the largest in the kitchen run again by a Demi-god with three commis, two trainee managers and two apprentices and even with its own porter.

Daily stocks were prepared, not just a general stock, but a brown beef stock that simmered for three to four days, a white stock that cooked till full of flavour from chicken carcasses and the numerous other daily made sauces such as the veal bones made into jus-lie, tomato sauce and béchamel all made with tender loving care. God help anyone who put anything into the stockpot without first checking with the saucier chef.

I was supposed to enjoy working with this Polish chef de partie. I do not believe that I am racist, but why were the Polish chefs the hardest to work for. I soon learnt that they were even harder and expected even more than the much-hated French Sous chefs who in turn seemed to dislike all chef de parties. "Could anyone ever turn this into a team?"

It was here that I discovered the "kitchen bible" from the almost violent arguments that aroused daily around the posted "plat du jour menu" which would end at the first court of appeal, "Le Répertoire de la Cuisine", and if that book did not settle the argument or the point scoring, recourse to the immortal Guide by Escoffier.

Also in the sauce corner, we learnt to look down on the loufiats, (waiters) who were the lowest of the low and even lower than the plongeur who washed the pots and pans.

My next yearn, like all the other apprentices, was to be assigned to the Pâtissiere where we would actually learn mostly by watching how to make sugar baskets, ice-cream bombes and, much more; the real secrets carefully being covertly hidden by the English Chef de partie.

Before my dream would become reality, I had a six month stint in the Entremetier. Here fingers would bleed from peeling bags of chestnuts, every evening making pan upon pan of pommes voison, sauté potatoes; that had to be exactly right; the epinards en branchs (or branched spinach), and other varieties of daily vegetables.

Prepared in a hell where slave labour was the norm and the only part of the day worth living was the daily ritual of playing poker each afternoon from 3 pm to 5 pm before returning to work, and all for 2 pounds 15 shillings a week.

But now, a one month rest, yes a holiday on the grill designed to make one sweat from morning to night in front of a charcoal grill. Does anyone really know how damn hot those things get? Filet mignon, point rump which must have the triangle fat, French cutlets, mixed grills and more, all turned over at the precise moment and poked with sticky fingers to ensure degree of doneness is perfect. Then a transfer to the fish section, second only in reputation to the sauce partie, and music to ones daily routine. Cooking at last; but no, polishing the copper pans with lemon juice and salt, making hollandaise twice daily. But now, in my second year, I have power!

I am in charge of another apprentice and damned hard he will work! "He is my slave and if I did not like it, he would do it", and if I ever wished to be amused, I will send him to the maintenance department for a left handed hammer or to put a shilling into the gas meter. Yes bliss; I am now powerful; I have finally tasted power and I like it!

At last, it is my third year and the "sweets" that really meant, burnt fingers from sugar, ice-cold hands, and working with an equally demanding Pâtissier. It was here that I learnt the lesson to enter competitions. "Voilá", my first silver medal at Earls Court, Salon Culinaire for what I believed was a perfect Charlotte Royale, displayed

history - my introduction into a commercial kitchen

amongst endless other charlottes that were awarded gold, however it was mine. I had won, I was king.

It was hard work in conditions that would not be acceptable today. At the time, I was "not happy, Jan" but, on reflection, thank goodness I could not change it. I had unknowingly learnt discipline, skills, respect and, more importantly, I discovered that before one can lead and give orders, one needs to learn how to take orders.

I suggest that whilst these old days are gone for good, I believe that our modern apprentices miss out on some real life skills.

I doubt very much if any modern apprentices, who often seem to have a self-inflated view of entitlement, would take the abuse, the conditions and the rate of pay. There again, how many of them learn to make basic sauces and extend them into hundreds of combinations; tell a degree of doneness of a roast from just looking at it; pull sugar; carve a carrot into a carnation and know how to decorate food in an elegant way.

How many apprentices experience the passion, the sense of duty, the daily urgency and soak it up like a sunny day; leaving work everyday with a fuzzy warm feeling?

I just thank God and the many Demi-Gods, that I was an apprentice in that era and welcome the reality.

Whatever you think you can do, or dream you can do, Begin it! Boldness has power and magic in it.

> This is my philosophy, written to encourage readers to thinkabout the future of the CHEF.
> Analyse its contents to form a clear and distinct understanding of its arguments.
> Then agree or disagree, but please don't shoot the messenger.

03. For goodness SAKE,

Are we cooks
or are we
chefs?

*We may live without poetry, music and art;
We may live without conscience
and live without heart;
We may live without friends;
We may live without books;
But civilized man cannot live without cooks*

Taken respectfully from a quotation by
Edward Robert Bulwer-Lytton, 1st Earl of Lytton (1831 - 1891)

What is the truthful and accurate meaning of the terms "COOK" and "CHEF"?

In many instances both titles are inappropriately used throughout the commercial cookery community, and tragically misinterpreted by many in the public arena.

The confusion between the meaning of the title cook and chef is apparent since the many pretenders to fit a self-inflated view of entitlement have hijacked the term "*Chef*"; and because they believe, the title "*Chef*" brings to the table creditability and respectability.

Anyone who prepares and cooks food for a living is a "*Cook*" and "*Chef*" is a clearly defined position of responsibility and experience.

The meaning is clearly acknowledged in many dictionaries where "*Cookery*" is described as the art and practice of cooking and a "*Cook*" is defined as a person who has studied the art and practice of cooking.

| for goodness sake, are we cooks or are we chefs

The name of the trade is "*Commercial Cookery*" and a person who has successfully studied commercial cookery is a cook. While at the same time the designation "*Chef*" is traditionally recognised in many countries as a skilled cook who is the sole manager of a commercial kitchen.

The etymology or historical derivation of the term "*Chef*" (in several languages and originally a French expression) translates to chief and therefore should be correctly used only to describe the supervisor of a commercial kitchen brigade.

There are some **Amazing Inaccurate Descriptions** such as:

An apprentice chef is an expression not found as a technical description in any acknowledged dictionary or technical manual. Subsequently, "*I am an apprentice chef*" is clearly misrepresentative, as one cannot train to be an apprentice chief.

The technically accurate title of a person training to develop into a chef is an "*Apprentice Cook*" or a trainee cook and employed in an "*Apprenticeship in cookery*". They are not an apprentice in cheffery, nor employed in the trade of cheffery.

Schools, colleges, and cookery institutes may well be doing more harm than good when advertising they teach students to be chefs.

They do not help the industry, nor their students, and only encourage a continuing misunderstanding of correct titles and career paths. Just as, "I am cheffing" when asked what one does for a living is illogical and nonsensical, it is akin to describing oneself as a manager, without qualifying where at, or what you actually manage.

Likewise, describing oneself as a chef is also technically inaccurate of one's career, unless the person's role is to manage a kitchen brigade, or is a part of the supervision process in a commercial kitchen.

Chef de partie is a metaphor for a supervisor cook, or the cook in charge of a team within a brigade. Chef de parties are still cooks by trade.

Chef de cuisine is a legitimate title when in charge of a kitchen brigade and Executive chefs, titled as such, only when responsible for multiple kitchen brigades. One cannot be an Executive chef when responsible for only one kitchen, no matter how large the brigade.

Sous chef or Executive Sous chef are justifiable titles, provided the person is actually the understudy to the head, or Executive chef.

Founded on inaccurate industry usage, there has been a community misunderstanding of the interpretation of the title "Chef "driven by self-interested people outside the real commercial kitchen or fanned by media hype to hijack the term for selfish commercial reasons.

Culinary institutions, mostly second rate, are as much to blame as anyone as they attempt to appeal to unaware clients and capture market share by falsely promoting they are teaching chefs.

The unfortunate outcome that is led by graduates, or the new age "pretender chefs", is to continue to take the wrong road by believing that once they attend a college or obtain a piece of paper from a training institute, "Voila", overnight they have metamorphosed into a real chef.

Even some cookery teachers have taken on pretentious titles such as chef educator or chef teacher and augmented the problem. They have forgotten, or worse, do not realise they are professional cookery teachers.

| for goodness sake, are we cooks or are we chefs

EVALUATE EACH SCENARIO IN THE
FOLLOWING CASE STUDIES TO AGREE OR
DISAGREE WITH THEIR RANK AND TITLE.

Scenario 1 : I am responsible for the food service in three properties; one is a restaurant with 12 in the kitchen brigade, another is a café in a public garden and I manage a leased food service bistro in a small hotel. Each of the properties has their own head chef.

 ....

In the case above, we have a cook who is responsible for a number of properties and manages other chefs, therefore is in a senior leadership position. A cook with leadership responsibility of more than one kitchen is an **Executive chef.**

Scenario 2 : I am 36 years old having enjoyed a total of 20 years in a commercial kitchen, my career commenced with an apprenticeship and worked my way up the ladder to have 48 staff within my brigade. I am responsible for seven apprentices and 30 others who cook on various shifts. My kitchen is open for 18 hours a day and seven days a week. I decide when the menus change, who we purchase products from, what dishes look and taste like, and manage a budget of over four million a year.

 ....

In this case, we have a cook who is responsible for all the cooks, as a manager of the kitchen. A cook with managerial responsibility in one kitchen is a **Chef de cuisine.**

Scenario 3: I work in a hotel with eight in the brigade; there is a Chef de cuisine, a Sous chef, and I run the larder. There are three apprentices and one is assigned to me.

In this situation, we describe a cook who is responsible for an apprentice, therefore in a leadership position. A cook with leadership responsibility is entitled to be called a **Chef.**

Scenario 4 : I have just successfully completed my college certificate and just commenced a new job in a restaurant working for a well-known chef. There are four in the kitchen, the Chef, Sous chef, a Garde-manger and I am responsible for entrées and sweets.

In this scenario, we have a cook who does not have responsibility for another and is not in a leadership position, therefore a **Cook**.

Scenario 4 : I am in my final year of training, having worked with two well-known chefs both in a fine dining restaurant. I am very confident that I will pass my final exams with credits, just as I did in the first two years.

In this case, we have a person in training who is an Apprentice or **Trainee cook.**

Scenario 5 : I was 16 years old last week. I have just left school to enjoy my part-time first job in a kitchen. During the week, I washed some garden greens and assisted the chef plate up the entrée for a function. I am passionate about my future and sure that one day I will lead a kitchen. I look forward to attending school soon.

| for goodness sake, are we cooks or are we chefs

*In this scenario, the title is **Food Service Assistant**.*

> **Scenario 6 :** *I have great cooking skills developed at home, and would love to become qualified in the commercial cookery world and yearn to one day own my own restaurant. I can memorize and produce a great dish from a recipe. I have demonstrated that I am creative with food preparation and appeared in a popular TV show.*

*A contestant remains a **Contestant**.*

> **Scenario 7 :** *I regularly present a TV program. Though I have never actually trained in or managed a commercial kitchen, I am very good with communication and demonstration skills, having a trained media background. I am considered by my substantial audience to be able to produce a great recipe.*

*What should my title be? **Domestic food demonstrator**.*

Others have sheepishly followed without the real understanding of either station or particularly the ethics required by the title or position for either cook or chef.

Celebrity chefs who do not have commercial cookery foundation or experience in a commercial kitchen are **domestic food demonstrators.**

Restaurant reviewers who imply they are chefs are **food media writers.**

Hospitality V.E.T teachers, some who are home economists are **secondary school cookery teachers.**

Cookery book writers, who are not trained or experienced in cookery, are by association identified as chefs when in reality they are **authors.**

There are others who demonstrate products in various activities sometimes wearing white poofy hats and selling something food related are really **product demonstrators.**

The distortion of the title chef is fuelled by bad employers, who need a qualified cook; then advertise for a chef, believing that to attract the right person they need to glorify their advertisement.

Additionally other derivatives that have added to the confusion yet have indisputable industrial meanings, include Master Chef and Chef de Rang.

We have long passed the technical and simplistic meaning of the term. We know the term chef originated from "Chief" and the term can technically be used to describe many "Chiefs". For example, a tram driver is a *Conducteur De Tramway,* or an orchestra conductor is a *Chef D'Orchestre.*

We know that the head of a commercial kitchen is by technical definition a Chef de cuisine and there are those described by their peers as a "Chef", mainly to acknowledge their past endeavours. This is appropriate, provided they still advocate the fundamental principles and ethics of the role.

Do you have the right to call yourself a chef? Or be addressed as a chef by your colleagues? What also is a cook? What is wrong with calling someone a cook, or calling oneself a cook? Is it, politically incorrect, bigoted, insulting, or even demeaning? On the other hand, is it that chefs do not understand a cook has and should have the same standing in the industry as a chef?

For example, if someone were to describe you as cook, would it bother you that they chose the term cook, rather than chef? I am curious for any opinions on this, as it appears that word "Cook" has become a dreadful four lettered word, and "Chef" signifies glamour and authority.

It may even be that we need to revolutionise the word chef to something else and agree on new titles such as Kitchen Director, Chef Director, or Kitchen Manager. In addition, leave those who believe that they are chefs to their own delusions.

So who is a Chef?

A cook becomes a chef when they have achieved defined core competencies, shown accepted attitudes, and values that have been derived from experience in a commercial cookery environment and assumed responsibility for the actions of another cook.

When all cores are achieved, a person should still be content to call himself or herself a cook and only when promoted to a supervisory role should they be titled a chef. I know many chefs who are proud to consider themselves primarily a cook, even though they qualify to be a chef.

Functioning as a cook or chef must be more than simple employment. Genuine cooks and chefs who have moved above "just a job" have realised their responsibilities to the community and industry and have joined the industry as a professional.

Cooks and chefs operate in a very stressful, complex, and demanding environment and daily push their minds and bodies, fuelled by a passion, attempting the almost impossible.

Successful chefs by their very nature are highly intelligent; fundamentally required to achieve the daily challenging tasks of purchasing, storing, legalities, food preparation, staff co-ordination, and the many other daily experiences of their environment.

Although chefs do not need to be initially well educated to be successful, education helps along the rocky road.

Even some highly successful chefs did not need formal training. They alternatively trained for many years as a kitchen assistant in a commercial kitchen under a skilled chef, gradually obtaining the skills, attitude, knowledge and experience required to eventually work their way up the kitchen ladder.

Clearly, to be a cook or chef and cope with the daily pressures, intelligence is mandatory for success.

A good education will definitely assist as it helps to develop natural intelligence in different ways and speed up the learning curve. A good education does not automatically lead to being a successful cook or chef, but a high degree of intelligence usually will.

One of the basic reasons why some chefs came out of a poor educational background and still achieved a renowned position is the known phenomenon that people of well above average intelligence sometimes do poorly in school due to boredom.

Never stir a Chef or you will end up being "FRIED"

Is stir-fry on the menu?

04. The SAKE Philosophy

Who is a
CHEF?

To identify the vital criteria that shape a cook or a chef, a philosophical model has been developed called:

The 'SAKE' Philosophy.

"For goodness SAKE, be like a cook or chef".

A substantial number of people who call themselves a chef or think they are a chef, are in fact not.

Being able to produce a simple dish or a limited range of meals does not make a person a cook or a chef.

Cooks and chefs are artisans, who must have four obligatory fundamentals:

> ➤ Expert practical skills.
>
> ➤ Definite common industry values.
>
> ➤ A comprehensive knowledge of food preparation beyond their immediate practice.
>
> ➤ Progressive participation in a commercial kitchen.

These fundamentals are identified as a Chef's 'SAKE'; or their **S**kills, **A**ttitude, **K**nowledge and **E**xperience.

This description was developed in an attempt to succinctly define and quantify the technical, conceptual and attitudinal requirements to be legitimately titled a cook or chef.

There has been much said about the misuse of the designation chef. Aside from the literal technical translation "Chef translating to Chief", the title is ambiguous in the community and even in some industry sectors.

To my knowledge, no one has ever attempted to define the complete physical and psyche of a cook/chef.

There are numerous brief descriptions of the occupation and as

the sake philosophy - who is a chef

many detailed verbose curricula that identify what should be taught for the job as a cook/chef.

However, what is additional to the basic skill set, what are the intrinsic characteristics and the supporting psychological factors that define a genuine cook/chef?

'SAKE' is a philosophy that advocates that four indispensable interconnected components must exist for a person to be a genuine cook or chef.

What a cook or chef can physically do:
summarised as **SKILLS**

The ideals, traits and passion inherent in a cook or chef:
summarised as **ATTITUDE**

The technical data a cook or chef must be familiar with:
summarised as **KNOWLEDGE**

The formative milestones required in a cooking career:
summarised as **EXPERIENCE**

Unless a person can demonstrate completeness and competency in **ALL FOUR** components, they are neither a cook or a chef.

Furthermore, a cook must be able to demonstrate supervisory responsibility in a commercial kitchen to be a Chef.

The following definitions are representative of a cook/chef **'SAKE'** who practices in a modern Australian or European cuisine commercial kitchen.

Skills, Attitude and Experience are global constants; other culinary cultures may use this model by replacing the knowledge components to reflect local requirements.

The questions are?

CAN YOU
Consistently procure, prepare and present food within the cost and time constraints in a quantity food production using foundation culinary preparations and techniques without a recipe?

ARE YOU
Innovative with and passionate about food?

DO YOU
Respect culinary history and know culinary terminology?

HAVE YOU
Sufficient commercial kitchen experience?

05.Skills

Physical and Conceptual Ability

A cook/chef who has the "skills" will consistently demonstrate confidence to technically procure, prepare, and present wholesome food within the cost and time constraints applicable to their work environment.

A capable cook/chef is:

Competent at selecting and safely using:
Basic knives that Bone, Carve, Chop, Cut, Dice, Fillet, Slice and Decorate.

Proficient with using small tools that are used to:
Ball, Beat, Blend, Brush, Cook, Decorate, Grate, Grind, Juice, Lift, Mash, Measure, Mix, Mould, Open, Peel, Pierce, Pound, Press, Purée, Roll, Saw, Scale, Scoop, Scrape, Sharpen, Shear, Shred, Sift, Spoon, Strain, Turn, Tenderise, Whisk and Zest.

Efficient with using small tools and equipment including:
Bowls, Can Opener, Chinoise, Colander, Corers, Cutting Board, Egg Slicer, Fish Slicers, Forks, Fry Pans, Grater, Kitchen Scissors, Ladle, Mandolin, Measuring Jugs, Mortar and Pestle, Pastry Bag, Potato Scoop, Rolling Pin, Saucepans, Scales, Scoops, Scraper, Sieves, Spatulas, Spiders, Spoons, Thermometers, Toasters, Tongs, Whisks and Zester.

Capable of safely using:
Bain-Marie, Benches, Blender, Boiler, Bowl cutter, Brat pan, Char Grill, Deep Fryer, Dishwasher, Floor Scales, Freezers, Fryers, Gravity Feed Slicers, Grill plate, Grills, Hot Press, Mechanical Peeler, Microwave, Ovens, Planetary Mixers, Refrigerators, Salamanders, Shelving, Steamers, Stockpot, and Stoves.

Practiced at applying techniques:
Blanch, Carve, Chop, Clean, Cream, Cut, Dice, En-robe, Grate, Knead, Layer, Mix, Peel, Pipe, Refresh, Roll, Segment, Shred, Slice, Temper, and Tie.

| skills - physical and conceptual ability

 Conversant with the use of:
The Methods of Cookery to prepare and present Appetisers, Cakes, Canapés, Cheese, Desserts, Dressings, Eggs, Farinaceous, Fish, Fruit, Game, and Hors d'oeuvre, Meat, Pastries, Poultry, Salads, Sandwiches, Shellfish, Soups, Sweets, Vegetables and Yeast Goods.

Skill and passion make an unbeatable team.

Successful cooks and chefs inherently have common characteristics that underpin their practical skills. They are:

 Aware of the need to:
Quickly identify and respond to difficult situations in a controlled manner without fault-finding at the time.

 Capable of functioning under stress and can:
Enjoy the experience of operating in a dynamic environment. Maintain a sense of humour under pressure. Stay calm and controlled in demanding situations. Stay focused when constantly faced with deadlines.

 Cautious and:
Aware of the potential physical and biological hazards in purchasing, storing, cooking and serving food for mass consumption.

 Good at Communication who:
Favour succinct assertive communication. Favour verbal communication. Have good listening skills. Operate their kitchen with clear and concise instructions. Realise that winning by bullying will lose the trust of others. Realise various cultures require different approaches.

 Physically fit who can:
Endure a highly active environment. Lift heavy boxes, pots and objects within legal limits. Stand on their feet for long periods. Withstand constant temperature changes.

Innovative and:
Able to modify traditional, classical or contemporary techniques to prepare and present novel, fashionable and appealing menus.

> ## *Are cooks and chefs creative or innovative? There is a basic difference between the two.*

Often promoted as one of the characteristics required by a cook or chef is having a creative streak, which by definition is inaccurate.

Being creative is attempting to establish something that did not previously exist. Being innovative is re-arranging the old in a new way. As the fundamental principles and methods of cookery and the products exist, chefs do not create, they rearrange.

Being successfully creative and entirely original with food is highly unlikely. Apart from the probability that someone else has thought of the combination before; one cannot sensibly create good food without the backdrop of proven skills, knowledge and experience.

Creativity is the realm of the untrained or inexperienced who have little or no understanding of the basic principles and methods required to prepare quantities of commercial food.

Any person can think of a thousand new ways of preparing foods in their mind and create absurd combinations, while not able to perceive their creations are foolish and unworkable.

Experienced chefs are innovative; they use foundation principles to fashion novel combinations, often using technology and exciting ways of presenting a new dish. They use the old to invent the new. They know from experience the new idea will gastronomically work, then refine and produce a new marketable dish.

It is the fundamental reason why understanding the basics is so important to being a successful cook or a chef.

06. Attitude

Characteristics
and
Personality
Traits

A cook/chef who has the "**Attitude**" will acknowledge there is more to being a cook or a chef than putting food on a plate and will instinctively be: *conscious of detail, focus on solutions not problems, is committed to excellence, notices the best features in others and is well mannered when dealing with people.*

The difference between a good and a great chef is often simply their attitude. A chef's attitude towards their responsibility will have a substantial controlling influence on their success, both on a daily basis and on their career.

Attitude is about the chefs' self-perception; about showing one is depressed or cheerful, it is demonstrated by the way the cook/chef domestically or professionally dress, groom themselves, talk, smile, work, show appreciation or respond to others on a daily basis. Their attitude demonstrates their commitment and delight in being a cook/ chef.

Ask a chef how they are and, if the answer is "EXCELLENT", the positive response encourages and motivates. As the conductor of the kitchen orchestra, (or their brigade) when the chef is negative, the brigade notices the negativity and quickly become depressed. They inherit the infectious tone that will result in increased stress and disjointed teamwork.

The kitchen is the second home of a chef, apart from their family, it is their life and passion; great chefs are adept at using their passion to excite and their attitude to motivate the brigade to excel. A cook or chef at any level with a positive attitude will gain the respect of others, and generally result in upward mobility.

Traits and characteristics commonly found among highly successful cooks and chefs:

- **Accountable for their actions:**
  Able to admit mistakes.
  Determined to deliver as required.

| attitude - characteristics and personality traits

- **Ambitious with a strong desire to achieve recognition:**
  Has high self-esteem.
  Has a personal career goal.
  Has a task-oriented personality.
  Is competitive.
  Set and expect high levels of personal performance.
  Welcomes the opportunity to take a leadership role.

- **Ethical in dealing with staff, suppliers and clients:**
  Avoids classical names on menus unless classically prepared. Is committed to environmentally friendly work practices.
  Is honest and reliable.
  Is loyal to their subordinates.
  Strives to empower staff to reach their full potential.

- **Self- disciplined with the ability to self - motivate:**
  Aware that service time is stressful on the entire brigade.
  Confident in their abilities and opinions.
  Physically hard workers.
  Persistent when faced with kitchen crisis or extraordinary demands. Realise that systemic readiness is the key to daily operation.

- **Mindful of the need to:**
  Acknowledge they are a paraprofessional.
  Adhere to legalisation that affects the commercial kitchen.
  Comply with the enterprise policies, standards and procedures. Follow customary culinary conventions and chefs' etiquette. Practice good personal hygienic habits.

- **Passionate about:**
  Food, particularly the sourcing of quality produce. Mentoring the futures industry.
  Openly sharing knowledge with others.
  Supporting training initiatives.
  What they daily do.

- **Added in the 'SAKE' philosophy:**
  (While many successful chefs possess these mindsets, others have neglected to observe these four crucial core values that constitute a true professional).

➤ Recognise the need to brand the profession by wearing a cooks/chef's uniform appropriately and particularly when in a public arena.

➤ Adhere to a code of professional conduct e.g. Codes of Practice. Chapter 22.

➤ Value continuous self-development.

➤ Join and network through chef's associations.

Negative characteristics often found in cooks and chefs:

✗ **Dogmatic:**
Developed from an environment where there are strict rules and utter obedience is expected, cooks and chefs tend to disregard the opinions of others.

✗ **Emotional:**
Chefs are usually very sensitive, their passion engenders very high personal expectations and, when disappointed; their emotions can develop into rage or emotional anger.

✗ **Egotistical:**
Confidence, passion and pride are great qualities however; an almost indefinable line separates these qualities from ego. Chefs tend to be egotistical because they are following a dream and a unique personal vision.

> *A CULINARY PARADOX.*
> *Stroke a cooks/chefs ego and you will soon have them eating out of your hand.*

> *Passion is a chefs' thermometer, it measures the heights that one can achieve.*

07. knowledge

essential theory
and
practical ability

A cook / chef who has the "KNOWLEDGE" is able to describe foundation culinary preparations, fundamental commercial cookery techniques, culinary terminology and the reaction of ingredients in preparation and cooking.

They will be able to identify and procure a wide variety of products and produce, prepare wholesome foodstuffs in commercial quantities, normally without a recipe, while being familiar with legalisation that applies to a commercial kitchen.

There are three basic progressive degrees of knowledge in a cookery career:

A Cook / Chef will have knowledge of:

- Basic theory
- Basic Calculations
- Butchery
- Cakes & pastries
- Canapes
- Sandwiches and Cheese
- Compliance Eggs and Farinaceous
- Environment and Sustainability
- Equipment and Tools
- First Aid
- Fish and Shellfish
- Food Presentation
- Global Culinary Terminology
- Herbs and Spices
- Hors d'oeuvre
- Hot and Cold Desserts
- Hygiene and HACCP
- Larder and Buffet
- Meat Cookery
- Menu planning
- Methods of Cookery
- Mise-en-place
- Nutrition
- Occupational Health and Safety
- Personal Development
- Popular Global Preparations
- Potato
- Poultry
- Product Knowledge
- Salads and Dressings
- Stock Soups and Sauces
- Sweets and desserts
- Vegetable
- Fungi and Fruit
- Yeast products

| knowledge - essential theory and practical ability

A Chef de cuisine will have additional knowledge of:
- Accounting
- Costing
- Budgeting
- Food Science
- In-Vogue
- Leadership
- Purchasing
- Stores Control

An Executive chef furthermore will be familiar with:
- Business Management,
- Advanced Communication Skills
- Food Service
- Human Resource
- And may require other business management skills

A Representative Sample that illustrates the basic knowledge required by a cook / chef:

BASIC THEORY ....
Theoretical and functional knowledge:
- Chef's Uniform
- Branding
- Culinary History
- Marie Antoine Carême
- Auguste Escoffier Fundamental Gastronomy
- Modern Kitchen Roles and Titles
- Food Presentation
- Heat Transfer
- Convection
- Conduction
- Radiation
- Kitchen Hierarchy
- Senses
- Modern and Classical Kitchen Organisation
- Methods of Preservation

BASIC CALCULATIONS ....
Theoretical and functional knowledge:
- Temperature controls for commercial kitchen appliances.

- Temperatures required for storing dry, fresh, frozen, meat, and perishables.

Able to calculate:

- Food Cost Percentage
- Food Cost
- Liquids And Weights
- Selling Price
- Extend Formulas And Recipes

BUTCHERY

Theoretical and functional knowledge:

Breakdown of carcass beef, lamb, pork, quality, storage, preparation, descriptions, and ham numbers:

> ***Beef:*** *Butt, Rump, Hindquarter, Forequarter, Primal Cuts, Shin, Topside, Silverside, Rump, Sirloin, Fillet, Chateaubriand, Filet Mignon, Noisette, Rib, Spareribs, Bolar and Oyster Blade.*

> ***Lamb:*** *Baron, Chop, Chump, Crown, Cutlet, Leg, Neck, Noisette, Rack, Rosettes, Saddle, Shank and Shoulder.*

> ***Pork:*** *Butterfly, Chop, Fillet, Hand, Leg, Loin, Shoulder.*

> ***Veal Cuts:*** *Escalopes, Chop, Cushion, Cutlet, Knuckle, Leg, Loin, Neck, Rump, Shoulder.*

> ***Goat:*** *Capretto, Leg, Saddle, Shoulder.*

> ***Game:*** *Buffalo, Crocodile, Emu, Hare, Kangaroo, Ostrich, Rabbit, and Venison.*

> ***Offal:*** *(Beef, Lamb, and Veal) Brains, Heart, Kidneys, Liver, Oxtail, Sweetbreads, Tongue and Tripe.*

CAKES AND PASTRIES

Theoretical and functional knowledge: Biscuits

- Cakes
- Pastries
- Yeast Goods
- Bouchée
- Choux Pastry
- Cream Puffs
- Croquembouche
- Danish Pastry
- Éclairs
- Friands

| knowledge - essential theory and practical ability

- Gâteau
- Torte
- Hot Water Pastry
- Macaroons
- Madeleine's
- Palmiers

- Puff Pastry
- Short Pastry
- Sponge
- Sweet Pastry
- Viennese Biscuits

Able to prepare commercial quantities:

- Apple Pie
- Cheese Cake
- Cheese Straws
- Choux Swans
- Cream Puffs
- Danish Pastries
- Génoise Sponge
- Profiteroles

- Puff Pastry
- Quiche Lorraine
- Sugar and Chocolate Cookery
- Short Pastry
- Cookery
- Sweet Pastry
- Tarte Tatin
- Viennese Biscuits

CANAPÉS, SANDWICHES, AND CHEESE ....
Theoretical and functional knowledge:

- Bases
- Biscuits
- Butters
- Compound Butters
- Dressings and Garnishes
- Fillings
- Finger-Food
- Types of Bread
- Varieties of Cheese

- Cheese Accompaniments
- Blue-Veined
- Cream
- Firm
- Fresh
- Hard
- Semi-Soft
- Soft

Able to prepare commercial quantities:

- Canapés
- Cheese Board
- Cheese Plate

- Sandwiches
- Bookmaker
- Club

- Conventional,
- Croque-Monsieur
- Open
- Pinwheel
- Toasted

COMPLIANCE..
Theoretical and functional knowledge:

- Food Safety, OH&S, workplace legislation and regulations that apply to a commercial kitchen

EGGS AND FARINACEOUS ....
Theoretical and functional knowledge:

- Associated Culinary Terms
- Cooking
- Preparation
- Presentation
- Procurement
- Quality
- Safety
- Storage, Variety of Eggs, Rice and Pasta

Able to prepare commercial quantities:

- Benedict
- Flat Omelette
- Fried
- Hard-Boiled
- Omelettes
- Scrambled
- Soft Boiled
- Soufflé Omelette
- Stuffed Eggs
- Boiled Rice
- Braised Rice
- Fried Rice
- Couscous
- Gnocchi
- Lasagne
- Noodles
- Pasta
- Polenta
- Ravioli
- Risotto
- Spaetzle
- Spaghetti

ENVIRONMENT AND SUSTAINABILITY..................
Theoretical and functional knowledge:

- Biodegradable Products
- Carbon Footprint
- E. P. A. Environmentally Friendly Practices
- Power Reducing Strategies
- Recycling Waste.

| knowledge - essential theory and practical ability

EQUIPMENT AND TOOLS
Theoretical and functional knowledge:

- Common Tools and Equipment used in food preparation, Cleaning, Safety, and Sanitation

Able to use Common small and large kitchen equipment, as example:

- Bain Marie
- Bowl Cutters
- Cookers
- Cooking Pans
- Cooking Pots
- Cutters
- Decorative Tools
- Deep Fryers
- Gastronorm Containers
- Grillers
- Hot Boxes
- Knives
- Mallet
- Mandolin
- Measuring Jugs
- Mixing Machines
- Moulds
- Ovens
- Salamanders
- Service Tools
- Slicers
- Steamers
- Water Baths

FIRST AID
Theoretical and functional knowledge:

- Contents of a typical First Aid Box, Kitchen first aid

Able to:
- Respond to Cuts, Burns, Electric Shock, Fall and Bleeding
- Identify Potential Hazards
- Implement Safety Precautions
- Respond in an Emergency and Apply Simple First Aid

FISH AND SHELLFISH
Theoretical and functional knowledge:

- Associated Culinary Terms
- Cleaning
- Cooking
- Cutting
- Preparation
- Presentation
- Procurement
- Quality

- Safety
- Storage
- Sustainability
- Crustaceans
- Finfish Flat Fish
- Molluscs.
- Commercial

Varieties of Common Sea and Freshwater Fish

Able to: identify Common Local Commercial Species of Fish and Shellfish

- Barramundi
- Flathead
- Salmon
- Snapper
- Trevally
- Trout
- Tuna
- Whiting
- Oysters
- Mussels
- Crayfish
- Prawns
- Other Locally Popular Commercial Fish and Shellfish

Clean and Cut:

- Cutlet (Darne)
- Delice
- Fillet (Suprême)
- Goujonettes
- Goujons
- Paupiette

Able to prepare commercial quantities:

- Baked
- Deep Fried
- Grilled
- Pan-Fried
- Poached
- Steamed
- Fish and Shellfish
- En Papillote
- Fish Farce
- Matelote
- Paner a l'anglaise
- Quenelles
- Skewered
- Court Bouillon

FOOD PRESENTATION

Theoretical and functional knowledge:

- Arrangement
- Balance
- Colour
- Containers and Plates
- Food Styles
- Height
- Portioning
- Shapes
- Textures
- Influence of Ambience on Presentation

| knowledge - essential theory and practical ability

Able to prepare and present a contemporary garnished:
- Buffet
- Plate
- Platter

GLOBAL CULINARY TERMINOLOGY...........................
Theoretical and functional knowledge of:

- Global Culinary Terms that a cook/chef would be expected to be familiar with appears in chapter 25 "Terminology - Chefs speak"
- Local and/or culture specific terminology would be added or substituted

HERBS AND SPICES ....
Theoretical and functional knowledge:

- Associated Culinary Terms
- Cooking
- Preparation
- Presentation
- Procurement
- Quality
- Safety
- Storage
- Variety of common herbs and spices used in a commercial kitchen

Able to recognise:

➤ **Herbs:** Basil, Bay Leaves, Chives, Coriander, Garlic, Ginger, Marjoram, Mint, Mustard, Oregano, Parsley, Rosemary, Sage, Tarragon, Thyme

➤ **Spices:** Cardamom, Cayenne, Chilli, Cinnamon, Cloves, Coriander, Cumin, Curry Powder, Dry Ginger, Nutmeg, Paprika, Pepper, Saffron, Turmeric and other common herbs and spices

HORS D'OEUVRE..
Theoretical and functional knowledge:

- Associated Culinary Terms
- Antipasto
- Classical Hors D'oeuvre
- Cooking
- Mezze
- Preparation
- Presentation
- Tapas and other Appetizers

Able to prepare commercial quantities:

- à la Grecque
- Blinis
- Caviar
- Cocktails
- Crudités
- Fruit
- Meat
- Quiche
- Salads
- Seafood
- Terrines
- Vegetables

HOT AND COLD DESSERTS
Theoretical and functional knowledge:

- Creams
- Custards
- Ganache
- Gelatine Desserts
- Ice Creams
- Meringue
- Mousse
- Pancakes
- Panna Cotta
- Quenelles
- Sorbets
- Soufflés
- Sugar Boiling

Able to prepare commercial quantities:

- Bavarois
- Beignets
- Cream Caramel
- Crème Pâtissière
- Hot and Cold Soufflés
- Ice Cream
- Meringue
- Piped Chocolate Filigree
- Piped Cream
- Rice Conde

HYGIENE AND HACCP
Theoretical and functional knowledge:

- Food Hygiene
- HACCP Principles
- HACCP Terms
- Personal Hygiene
- Rules for Handling and Storage of Food

Able to prepare: Food Safety Plan.

LARDER AND BUFFET
Theoretical and functional knowledge:

- Buffet Types
- Cold Larder Preparations
- Garnishes
- Show Platters
- Portion Control
- Small Goods and Smorgasbord

Able to prepare commercial quantities:

- Chicken
- Fish

| knowledge - essential theory and practical ability

- Meat & Vegetable Platters
- Galantine
- Garnishes
- Mousse
- Pâté
- Salads
- Socles
- Terrines

MEAT COOKERY ....
Theoretical and functional knowledge:

- Cooking
- Degrees of Doneness
- Descriptions
- Preparation
- Quality and Storage

Able to: Apply the methods of cookery to the appropriate cut of meat.

Able to prepare commercial quantities:

- Blanquette
- Bolognaise
- Carbonnade
- Chateaubriand
- Chops
- Crown
- Crumbed Brains
- Curry
- Cutlets
- Escalope
- Filet Mignon
- Fillet Steak
- French Cutlets
- Fricassée
- Grilled Steak
- Hamburgers
- Kidneys
- Knuckle
- Lamb Fry
- Lamb Rack
- Liver & Bacon
- Meat Pie
- Medallion
- Moussaka
- Neck
- Noisette
- Osso Bucco
- Sweetbreads
- Shish Kebab
- Rib Roast
- Roast Bbq
- Rosettes
- Rump Steak
- Rump
- Sausages
- Sauté
- Schnitzel
- Shanks
- Rack
- Sirloin
- Spare Ribs
- Stroganoff
- Oxtail
- Tongue
- Topside
- Tournedos
- Tripe

MENU PLANNING ....
Theoretical and functional knowledge:

- Menu Planning Principles
- Client Mix
- Pricing Structures
- Terminology
- Prohibited Foods for Specific Groups
- Trends

- Types
- Compiling an:
  à la Carte, Table D'hôte, Cycle, Function, Theme, Breakfast Menu, Portion Control, Dietary and Religious Rules, Yield Testing, Standard Recipes
- Definitions

Able to compile: An à la Carte, cycle and set menu.

METHODS OF COOKERY..
Theoretical and functional knowledge:

- Principles of Baking
- Boiling
- Braising
- Deep Frying
- Grilling
- Microwave
- Poaching
- Poêléing
- Roasting
- Shallow Frying
- Steaming
- Stewing

Able to:

- Bake
- Boil
- Braise
- Deep Fry
- Grill
- Microwave
- Poach
- Poêlé
- Roast
- Shallow Fry
- Simmer
- Steam
- Stew a product

MISE-EN-PLACE..
Theoretical and functional knowledge:

The application of "Mise-en-place" in food production.

Able to prepare commercial quantities:

- Batters
- Bouquet Garni
- Brunoise
- Chop Parsley
- Château
- Compound Butters
- Croûtons
- Dice Onion
- Duxelles
- Frangipane
- Jardinière
- Julienne
- Macédoine
- Marinades

| knowledge - essential theory and practical ability

- Mirepoix
- Panada,
- Paner a l'anglaise
- Paysanne
- Printaniere

- Slicing Onion
- Studded Onion
- Stuffing's
- Tomato Concassé
- Yorkshire Pudding

NUTRITION ....
Theoretical and functional knowledge:

- Alcohol
- Carbohydrates
- Common allergies
- Diet rules
- Fibre
- Food groups
- Food standards

- Lipids
- Minerals
- Nutritional guidelines
- Proteins
- Special Diets
- Vitamins

OCCUPATIONAL HEALTH AND SAFETY........................
Theoretical and functional knowledge:

- Accident Book
- Accident Prevention
- Evacuation Procedures

- Fire Prevention
- Kitchen Safety
- Operating Dangerous Equipment

Able to safely:

- Use Kitchen Appliances
- Tools and Equipment
- Fire Extinguishers

- Blankets
- Carry Heavy Items
- Cut and Cook Foods

PERSONAL DEVELOPMENT ....
Theoretical and functional knowledge:

- Networking
- Salon Culinaire
- Professional Associations

- Ethics
- Conventions
- Social Media

POPULAR GLOBAL PREPARATIONS
Theoretical and functional knowledge:

- Antipasto
- Biryani
- Bouillabaisse
- Falafel
- Garam Masala
- Haggis
- Hangi
- Kimchi
- Matelote
- Nasi Goreng
- Pad Thai
- Paella
- Palou
- Spanokopita
- Sushi
- Tapas
- Tapenade
- Teriyaki
- Tom Yum
- Vindaloo
- Yum Cha

Able to prepare commercial quantities:

- Antipasto
- Curry
- Gravlax
- Kiev
- Moussaka
- Saltimbocca
- Tempura

POTATO
Theoretical and functional knowledge:

- Associated Culinary Terms
- Cooking
- Preparation
- Presentation
- Procurement
- Quality
- Safety
- Storage of common Varieties

Able to prepare commercial quantities:

- Boulangère
- Château
- Croquette
- Dauphine
- Duchesse
- French Fried
- Galette
- Gaufrette
- Matchstick
- Mignonette
- Noisettes
- Parisienne
- Straw

| knowledge - essential theory and practical ability

POULTRY
Theoretical and functional knowledge:

- Associated Culinary Terminology
- Cooking
- Cuts
- Boning
- Carving
- Grades
- Preparation
- Presentation
- Quality
- Storage: Chicken, Duck, Guinea Fowl, Pheasant, Pigeon, Quail, Squab and Turkey

Able to: Bard, Lard, Truss and cut a Chicken For Sauté

Able to prepare commercial quantities:

- Ballontine
- Coq au Vin
- Forcemeat
- Parmigiana
- Poussin
- Roast
- Sauté

PRODUCT KNOWLEDGE
Theoretical and functional knowledge:

- Availability
- Purchasing
- Quality
- Sizes
- Convenience Foods
- Basic Wine
- Dry Goods,
- Perishables.
- Storage of Local Produce and Supply Services

SALADS AND DRESSINGS
Theoretical and functional knowledge:

- Simple and composite salads.

Able to prepare commercial quantities:

- Beetroot
- Coleslaw
- French
- Mayonnaise
- Potato
- Roquefort dressing
- Thousand Island
- Vinaigrette
- Waldorf

STOCK SOUPS AND SAUCES

Theoretical knowledge:

- Preparation of Sauces
- Soups
- Stocks
- derivatives

Able to prepare commercial quantities:

- COLD SAUCES: Cocktail, Tartare.
- MISCELLANEOUS SAUCES: Apple, Bread, Horseradish, Mint, Sweet
- SOUR SAUCES (Emulsified): Béarnaise, Beurre Blanc, Hollandaise
- SAUCES: Béchamel, Bordelaise, Demi-Glace, Espagnole, Jus-Lie, Mornay, Tomato, Velouté.
- SOUPS: Bisque, Broth, Clarified, Cream, Gazpacho, Purée, Velouté, Vichyssoise
- STOCKS: Brown, Chicken, Fish and White Beef
- SWEET SAUCES: Crème Anglaise, Crème Pâtissière, Sugar Syrup
- THICKENERS: Roux, Blond, Brown, Beurre Manié

SWEETS AND DESSERTS

Theoretical and functional knowledge:

- Baba
- Charlotte
- Clafoutis
- Compote
- Coupe
- Dacquoise
- Frangipane
- Gelato
- Granite
- Junket
- Marzipa
- Sorbet
- Tiramisu
- Trifle
- Vacherin
- Zabaglione

Able to prepare commercial quantities:

- Baked Rice Pudding
- Bavarois
- Beignets
- Boil Sugar
- Crème Anglaise
- Conde
- Crème Brûlée
- Crème Chantilly, Ganache
- Ice Cream
- Ice Soufflé
- Meringue

| knowledge - essential theory and practical ability

- Mousse
- Soufflé
- Crépe
- Pancakes
- Poach Fruit

- Praline
- Sorbet
- Sugar Syrup
- Tuile

VEGETABLES, FUNGI AND FRUIT ....
Theoretical and functional knowledge:

- Associated Culinary Terms
- Cooking
- Preparation
- Presentation
- Variety: Bulb, Leaf, Leaf stalk, Root, Stem and Tuber Vegetables, Button, Chanterelle, Crimini, Enoki, Field, Morel, Oyster, Porcini, Portobello, Shiitake and Truffle Fungi
- Soft, Hard, Stone, Citrus and Tropical Fruits

- Procurement
- Quality
- Safety
- Storage

Able to prepare commercial quantities:

- Cauliflower Mornay
- Frozen Peas
- Glazed Carrots
- Poached Fruit
- Purée Spinach

- Ratatouille
- Sauté mushrooms and other common Vegetable
- Fungi and Fruit Accompaniments

YEAST PRODUCTS ....
Theoretical and functional knowledge:

- Fermentation
- Proofing

- Chemical
- Yeast leavening, formulas

Able to prepare commercial quantities:
Bread rolls, Pizza base

A Chef de cuisine will have additional knowledge of:

ACCOUNTING, BUDGETING, COSTING ....
Theoretical and functional knowledge:

- Budgets
- Cash Flow
- Records
- Profit and Loss Statements
- Accounting Software
- Cost Control
- Stock Control
- Standard Recipes
- Pricing Methods

Able to:

- Take Stock
- Read financial reports
- Price a menu
- Coach Staff
- Theoretical knowledge
- Competency Training
- External sources of training
- Training
- Principles

FOOD SCIENCE ....
Theoretical and functional knowledge:

- Enzymes in Cooking
- Role / Uses of Acids and Alkali
- Properties of Starch
- Glucose,
- Starches
- Emulsions and Stabilisers
- Structure of Proteins
- The Role of Gluten
- Properties of Gelatine
- Salt
- Caramelisation
- Chocolate
- Cheese making
- Basic Wine Styles
- Gluten
- Oxidisation
- Yeast and leavening agents

| knowledge - essential theory and practical ability

IN VOGUE
Theoretical and functional knowledge:
- Sources of information
- Culinary Magazines
- Trends
- Events

LEADERSHIP
Theoretical and functional knowledge:
- Culinary innovation
- Evaluative systems
- Information technologies
- Styles of leadership
- Autocratic
- Participative
- Delegation
- Quality controls
- Total Quality Management

PURCHASING, STORES CONTROL
Theoretical and functional knowledge:
- Stock Control
- Stocktaking
- Receiving

An Executive chef furthermore will be familiar with:

BUSINESS MANAGEMENT
Theoretical and functional knowledge:
- Business Model Planning
- Business Structures
- Culinary Industry Etiquette and Conventions
- Developing Goals
- Financing
- Hazard Management
- Marketing

FOOD SERVICE
Theoretical and functional knowledge:
- Basic Food and Beverage Service
- Advanced Communication Skills Theoretical and functional

knowledge:
- ~ Body Language
- ~ Communication Barriers
- ~ Disagreements and Complaints
- ~ Customer Relations
- ~ Information Technology
- ~ Listening Skills
- ~ Negotiation
- ~ Oral and Verbal Instructions

HUMAN RESOURCE MANAGEMENT
Theoretical and functional knowledge:

- Continuous Improvements
- Creating Cultures
- Induction Programs
- Job Descriptions
- Meetings procedures
- People Management
- Performance Appraisals

COMPLIANCE
Theoretical and functional knowledge:

Legislation related to:

- Advertising
- Contracts
- Guarantees
- HACCP
- Health and Safety
- Public Relations, Purchasing
- Small Claims Tribunal
- Workplace Relations

THE CONTEMPORARY COOK/CHEF NEED TO BE INNOVATIVE.

Training programs are often criticised by industry for including classical preparations, techniques and dishes. These comments are unwarranted. A foundation knowledge based on classical basics is essential for sensible innovation. Cooks and chefs must master the classical basics to be able to twist them properly.

> *Upward mobile executive chefs who seek senior management roles should commence graduate studies.*

08. experience

obligatory

commercial

participation

A cook/chef who has the "Experience", earns a livelihood (or germinated) from a commercial cooking career, with progressive and systematic guidance from a higher qualified chef in a commercial kitchen involving the following stages of development:

FOOD SERVICE ASSISTANT.

A general assistant mainly responsible for cleaning and back-up duties - Adept and gifted **may** eventually become a cook.

Also known as a: Kitchen assistant / kitchen hand

APPRENTICE COOK (ENTRY LEVEL)

Requires four years of formative kitchen practice in combination with a formal training program to develop into a cook or chef.

Also known as a: Trainee Cook / Commis cook / Stagiaire

COOK

Requires an accredited commercial cookery qualification and four years commercial kitchen experience as a trainee.

Or

Requires (without a recognised formal cookery qualification) A minimum of seven years commercial kitchen experience, **and** the influence of at least two trained chefs in separate properties.

Also known as a: Qualified cook / Station cook

CHEF

A cook who is the immediate supervisor of another cook or trainee.

Benchmark experience: Five years commercial kitchen practice.

Also known as a: Chef de partie / Qualified Chef

| experience - obligatory commercial participation

♙ SOUS CHEF.

A chef who is the second in command in the kitchen.

Benchmark experience: Nine years commercial kitchen practice.

Also known as a: Second Chef

♙ CHEF DE CUISINE

Responsible for the operation of a commercial kitchen: Benchmark experience: Ten years commercial kitchen practice.

Also known as a: Head Chef

♙ EXECUTIVE CHEF

Responsible for the operation of two or more commercial kitchens.

Benchmark experience: 15 years commercial kitchen practice.

Also known as a: Corporate Chef / Culinary Director

SCHOOLING

Cooks primarily obtain their experience on the job under the supervision of an experienced chef. This experience is customarily enhanced by formal classroom instruction in a cookery-training program in a college, private trainer, school or private provider that teaches the technical aspects necessary to achieve the tasks to an industry standard.

Off the job training programs, or commercial cookery courses, certifies that the student has achieved the minimum experiences to be a cook. However, a culinary qualification does not and cannot replace the crucial kitchen experience especially across a variety of properties.

Effectively, a cookery qualification accelerates the learning process and facilitates mobility. Mobility is vital to a chef who needs to be nomadic in their formative years to develop their **'SAKE'**.

There are many essential considerations to assess the worth of a qualification and one is time. The quality of a training program and the worth of its qualification is time-based insofar as there are a minimum number of hours required to teach the discipline properly. Everyone learns at a different pace, many different qualifications and modes of delivery exist. However, the recommended benchmark time to teach the minimum technical skills and knowledge to be a mobile cook in a dedicated quality culinary focused training program is between 720 and 860 notional contact hours.

Further, a course of study must include more than just technical skills and knowledge. The course must contain additional abstract further education subjects that aims to develop attitudes. This component will add to the course and may vary considerably.

Additionally the course content needs reinforcing in a quality industrial working environment under the guidance of a qualified chef over a minimum of four years of kitchen experience (Approximately 6000 hours of industrial practical kitchen experience).

Evidence indicates that qualified cooks with this minimum level of quality formal and industry training are globally mobile and well received.

One can teach a person to make an omelette in an hour, that does not make them a mobile cook, take six weeks to teach them mise-en-place, that does not make them a cook, or program a course for any number of hours under the benchmark, that in all probability is also inadequate.

If 360 hours of training is required to gain a qualification, there is a very good reason to believe it has only covered 50% of the skills and knowledge required by a mobile qualified cook. Just as, if a person only has two years industry experience in a kitchen, no matter

| experience - obligatory commercial participation

how gifted, they are ill-prepared to assume a fully qualified cook's position.

A simple method to establish the creditability of a culinary course or school is to consider their advertisements. Avoid educational institutes with websites or advertising material with images of students inappropriately dressed, or without hats, or those who advertise introductory training for chefs not cooks. This demonstrates a *fundamental misunderstanding* of the industry they service.

Logically a "Student Chef" is a misleading description, *students are trainee cooks*, they are learning to cook and do not have anyone reporting to them. As they are not responsible for the actions of others, they are *student cooks* **not** *student chefs*.

Courses should include final external practical assessment of students. Programs that include external final examinations have consistently produced better skilled graduates and higher achievers. It is not the examination in itself. Essentially the motivation to pass the final examination drives students to reach greater levels.

For gifted people who naturally adapt to cookery and never attend a formal training course of study normally require between six years to seven years on stove/commercial kitchen experiences (a minimum of 12000 hours of practical experience).

Two conditions apply, they must be highly motivated and their industry practice must be across multiple properties under the supervision of many chefs.

Evidence indicates that this unschooled pathway can develop a reasonably capable cook, though with rare exception, mobility will be a major issue in their career and particularly their capacity to achieve higher status as a chef.

An unschooled person needs multiple kitchen experiences to compensate for their lack of formal education. For example, a novice who purchases a restaurant, researches a menu and operates their own kitchen (even one that turns out to be highly successful) is not a cook or chef; they are a restaurateur who operates their own kitchen (Driving a car does not qualify one to be a mechanic).

Their skills and knowledge are not broad enough to be a mobile cook or a chef and, until they expand their experience in other properties, or work with trained chefs, their mobility is extremely limited.

An apprentice chef cooks in a fool's paradise

Observations

■

It is not logically possible to be a chef unless you are a cook first. A chef is a cook who has additional responsibility for the actions of another cook; therefore, **the fundamental and only difference between a cook and a chef is one of leadership.**

Broadcast and print media editorials and programs often show that producers and editors do not understand the correct description of a cook or chef and often misleadingly portray people to the public as chefs when they are neither a cook nor chef.

Once achieving genuine status of chef, using **'SAKE'** as a measurement, one is always a chef. Managers, sales, and other career paths where people evolved from a chef career inherit the title at the last or highest rank achieved as a working chef.

| experience - obligatory commercial participation

Competency Based Training

As theoretically sound as competency-based training appears to be, there are serious issues with competency training as a commercial cookery-training strategy. The apparent declining level of technical skills and knowledge among young cooks and chefs indicates that competency-based training strategy has failed to meet the needs of the commercial cookery industry in Australia.

> The notion that once a student demonstrates their ability to do something at school they are commercially competent is contrary to the traditional way a cook learns to perfect their skills at an industry standard and speed.

> Techniques learnt at school can be achieved in small quantities or under strict classroom conditions, but still require substantial practice to make perfect. Competency at school does not necessarily equate to being industry ready, which is the expectation of the model and a major reason why there is a shortage of skilled cooks.

> Compounding the issue, teachers are required to spend a disproportionate time in assessment at the expense of expanding and further exploring the subject matter in the classroom.

> Cooks are usually highly intelligent people, who often enter into the work force not as well educated as required by many other technical disciplines. Subsequently they are ill-equipped to handle a learner-focused approach.

> Teaching to a mastery level in cookery is relative; as principally who considers the standard of mastery? Particularly as businesses vary considerably in the industry.

> The notion of achieving mastery at "enterprise standard" used to express the minimum required standard to achieve competency is woefully inadequate to cope with cookery training; consequently, the competency training path has forced mastery of skills down to the lowest common denominator.

> Standards' committees and employer advisory groups predominantly comprised of larger properties are often biased in their advice on curriculum content. Particularly, the view of the small employer sector is ill-considered in syllabus design audits; resulting in the curriculum that is at variance with smaller restaurant and eating- places' needs.

The notion advocated by some education authorities in Australia that a certificate two equates to a qualified cook and a certificate three is a qualified chef, is WRONG AND MISLEADING. A cook is the qualification and a chef is a status. Chef is NOT a qualification. A certificate three is the minimum required to be a qualified cook and, in industry, a qualified cook REQUIRES SUPERVISORY EXPERIENCE to be a chef.

The mastery using a knife, is an extension of the chefs' personality.

| experience - obligatory commercial participation

Are you a cook, a chef ?
CHECKLIST

Can demonstrate: **YES / NO**
SKILLS identified in chapter five.

Agree with and adhere to fundamental: **YES / NO**
ATTITUDE principles identified in chapter six.

Have the theoretical and practical culinary: **YES / NO**
KNOWLEDGE identified in chapter seven.
(Check culunary terminology before self assesing this element)

Able to document culinary: **YES / NO**
EXPERIENCE identified in chapter eight to show a commercial cookery qualification based on a minimum of 720 hours of culinary training? And four years commercial kitchen experience.

Or

Have at least seven years commercial cookery experience in multiple properties with trained chefs.

'SAKE' Scores:

All four **YES** - **CONFIRMS A COOK**. Any No - <u>Not yet a cook.</u>

As a cook, do you supervise another person in the kitchen.
If <u>Yes</u> - **YOU ARE A CHEF.**

For a chef with a proven **'SAKE'**:

➤ Who is the second in command in a commercial kitchen.
If <u>Yes</u> - *You are a **Sous chef.***

➤ Who is responsible for the supervision of a kitchen.
If <u>Yes</u> - You are a ***Chef de cuisine.***

➤ Who manages two or more commercial kitchens.
If <u>Yes</u>- You are an ***Executive Chef.***

09. titles

culinary
titles and
ranks

Fundamentally;

A trainee or an apprentice is learning to use their hands to become a qualified cook.

A qualified cook has learnt to use their hands and now is learning to use their brain in order to progress to a Sous chef.

A Sous chef has learnt to use their hands and brain and is learning to use other- Hands to advance to a Chef de cuisine.

A Chef de cuisine has learnt tb use their hands; their brain, other hands and is learning to use other brains to mature as an Executive chef.

An Executive chef is simply a cook who has learnt to use their hands and brains and other hands and brains.

Within the commercial kitchen.

While the classical hierarchical system is still completely relevant in larger brigades, the administration of the majority of commercial kitchens has dramatically changed. The classical brigade was washed down the sink long ago, notwithstanding some classical titles remain and many have becoming ambiguous. This includes the basic ranks: cook, and chef.

Unfortunately, the original portrait of the term cook as a skilled food preparation specialist and a chef as a highly skilled kitchen administrator is almost abandoned and means very little now compared to the community perception of a decade or more ago.

The millions of meals prepared daily in homes, mixed with the popularity of celebrity chefs, numerous foodie magazines and even the films like "Ratatouille" suggests that anyone can in fact cook.

Unfortunately, by fashionable public perception the title "cook" equates to a "chef", even if a person can only read a recipe and

titles - culinary titles and ranks

produce any sort of a meal they are unfortunately regarded as worthy of being a chef.

Included in the poisonous recipe are the numerous TV programs and print media editorials that have contributed by diluting the real meaning of the term, and status of a "chef". Today it seems anyone can be a chef, or, even God forbid, by innuendo a "Master Chef"!

Cooks and chefs need to be concerned about the general public perception of the title Chef. A rank and title that should portray a trained craftsperson capable of preparing healthy, nutritious, commercially viable, quality food in large quantities; that has sadly deteriorated to the extent that it can be symbolized by the image of a pretender who wears no head covering, a T-shirt, and a striped butcher's apron.

The adulteration of the term started when cooks believed that "Chef" increased their status within the community. Employers are just as guilty by advertising ambiguous, more impressive job titles as an alternative to promotion and used as a substitute for salary increases.

The domino effect resulted in Sous chefs who pretentiously delighted in being considered an "Executive Sous chef", while being responsible for two cooks, two apprentices, and one kitchen attendant in a small kitchen where careless opening of the kitchen front door can break the window at the back of the kitchen!

Even the term "Chef de cuisine" is often misconstrued, especially when irresponsible Chefs de cuisine identify themselves as an "Executive chef", *(in most cases not knowing what the title really means)*, to administer multiple full-time kitchens.

In addition, the worst of all modern inappropriately used titles would have to be "apprentice chef", who really is an apprentice cook or trainee cook as they have not yet completed their training, or supervised another person in the kitchen.

Even if they claim to supervise a lower level apprentice, given their training status, they should not be in that position. This misleading title has encouraged a sense of entitlement far beyond their capability.

Foundation Etymology

In professional cookery terms "chef" is derived and abbreviated from the French technical term "Chef de cuisine" or kitchen chief (French "chef" English "chief ') or the person in charge. As in: "Chef de cuisine", or the chief in charge of a single kitchen.

Apart from valid supervisory responsibilities, the term "chef" has the same meaning and connotation as "cook" and, as both require the same foundation and development, it follows that all chefs are primarily cooks.

Traditionally most titles in a kitchen related to their specific role in bringing together a meal. The globally respected original model was developed by the father of commercial cooking; Auguste Escoffier, who laid down the foundation of the classic partie system and kitchen titles; a fish cook cooked fish and a soup cook cooked soups, etc.

The classical classification of kitchen hierarchy does not consider titles or positions beyond Chef de cuisine, despite this limit; the contemporary commercial cookery industry has added many new titles and career opportunities for chefs.

Countless positions and chef titles are now outside the traditional kitchen structure, parties have amalgamated, and various senior chef positions go beyond the conventional Chef de cuisine level of responsibility. Chefs may now be responsible for multi property operations and chef positions exist in research, sales, education and more.

Faced with the extensive newly created titles such as corporate chef, culinary director, group chef, executive chef among the growing list that abound the industry, the public has become confused.

| titles - culinary titles and ranks

What do the new titles really mean?

The new titles exist exclusively in a corporate entity and the role and responsibility identified in a job description. As they are not able to be ranked or categorised, new or unusual titles are potentially subject to ambiguity and misinterpretation.

It is illogical to use industrial titles to determine culinary ranks, as this may result in infinite and confusing hierarchical culinary levels and conceivably subject to corrupt naming practices. *For example: Director of culinary may well become senior director of culinary, that potentially could evolve into chief executive of culinary etc, as each title attempts to increase the perceived status of the role.*

Corporations best describe the title of a role and the unique position described in their position description, notwithstanding, there is an industrial need for general categorisation into logical ranks.

A culinary rank is defined as the minimum level of skills, attitude, knowledge and experience required as a chef to discharge the basic culinary duties of the culinary role.

Depending upon the level of expertise, the position may require more than 'SAKE' evaluation. A senior culinary director may require an MBA to fulfil the job requirements; 'SAKE' is, however, the absolute minimum culinary expertise required as a chef.

The 'SAKE' philosophy addresses the confusion and contradictions that have arisen from the growth in new occupations, and by using a logical classification describes to the public the level of culinary expertise and responsibility that is required for any position (or title) that employs a chef.

The philosophy follows traditional classifications, only expanding, making them clearer and systematic.

Culinary ranks (may also be titles) primarily describe the administrative influence of the chef in or external to a kitchen. An example is Chef de cuisine (Rank) and their (Role) is the "Chief of the kitchen" or Chef de cuisine.

Many unique culinary titles describe roles that may be external to a commercial kitchen. An example is professional cookery teacher. The teacher is required to have achieved a rank in a kitchen prior to their appointed role. They were a qualified chef (Rank) and now a commercial cookery teacher (Role).

With the amalgamation of many of the parties and the multi-tasking of a contemporary cook's role, it may be more appropriate in the 21st century to consolidate titles and describe kitchen ranks and titles in terms of the authority and influence of the person.

The 'SAKE' philosophy proposes there are six culinary ranks (Categories) with every industry title aligned technically with one of the ranks. The level of influence of a person determines their culinary rank. For example, a person with the title corporate chef who manages multiple kitchens has the rank Executive chef. Their job title remains the same.

Depending upon the influence of supervising one kitchen or managing multiple kitchens, a chef manager, research and development chef, food and beverage chef, culinary team leader etc, would either be ranked as a Chef de cuisine or an Executive chef.

The six 'SAKE' ranks (Categories) are:

	RANK	INFLUENCE IN A KITCHEN
1.	Food Service Assistant	*Comply with instructions.*
2.	Apprentice cook	*Practice as instructed.*
3.	Cook / Chef	*Accomplish as required.*
4.	Sous chef	*Enforce kitchen policies.*
5.	Chef de cuisine	*Supervise a kitchen.*
6.	Executive chef	*Manage a cluster of kitchens.*

These descriptions do not in any way attempt or even suggest replacing the parti system, which for decades has classified chef's roles. All this philosophy does, is augment the classical system, and updates titles that did not originally exist placing them into understandable and logical categories.

| titles - culinary titles and ranks

Rank Descriptions

Rank 1
Food Service Assistant

Common position descriptions:
- Kitchen assistant.
- Kitchen attendant.
- Kitchen hand.

A Food Service Assistant is an unqualified culinary labourer who simply **COMPLIES** with instructions under the direct authority of a chef, their authority and influence is nil, as their fundamental role and position is, **"Yes chef"**

Many aspire to become a cook, and technically may become a cook when accepted into a commercial cook's position, usually after a number of years on the job experience. Nevertheless, in doing so are very limited in their professional upward mobility due to lack of technical education.

Their duties are to assist the chef with preparation, cooking and presentation of appetizers, soups, meats, vegetables, desserts, general kitchen cleaning and respond:

YES CHEF.

> **RECOMMENDED:**
> to attend a recognised food handling course.

The 'SAKE' philosophy will never prevent false claims, 'SAKE' is a measurement of reality

Rank 2
Apprentice cook

Common position descriptions:
- Trainee cook
- Commis cook
- Stagiaire

The conventional start on the hierarchical ladder and is a person learning the trade who **PRACTISES** instructions issued by the chef.

They attend school while working and become a qualified cook following successful completion of their culinary studies and indentured period.

Similar to a Food Service Assistant, an apprentice cook's influence in the kitchen is minimal, accepting they have a rightful expectation to learn the full range of practical skills at work and anticipate becoming a cook/chef upon graduation.

Once certified at school and with the practical kitchen experiences, they are upwardly mobile and usually nomadic in search of alternative career experiences.

REPORTS TO: Chef de Cuisine, Sous chef, Chef de partie, or immediate supervisor chef.

Typical function and progressively developing expertise:
- Under supervision prepare menu items

Under supervision comply with:
- Budgetary policies
- Food preparation policies
- Food presentation policies
- Hygiene practices
- Legislative Compliance

MANDATORY REQUIREMENT:
is to attend a recognised cookery training program.

| titles - culinary titles and ranks

Rank 3
Apprentice cook

Common position descriptions:
- Chef de partie
- Station cook or Chef
- Qualified cook or chef
- Or Classical partie title, e.g: Garde manger, pâtissier etc.

A Cook/Chef who unassisted **ACCOMPLISHES** as required.

Depending upon leadership requirements of the position, the correct industry title is either cook or chef. Technically a cook becomes a chef when given the responsibility to supervise the actions of another person and only then should they be identified as a chef. They inherit the basic title chef, as they are a semi - supervisor.

REPORTS TO: Sous chef or Chef de cuisine and in very small kitchens may work alone.

Typical function and obligatory knowledge:
- Independently prepare menu items

Able to comply with:
- Budgetary policies
- Food preparation policies
- Hygiene practices.
- Food presentation policies
- Hygiene practices
- Legislative Compliance

Must include the ability to:
- Perform the duties of a lesser role
- Supervise trainees.
- Check deliveries

RECOMMENDED TO: attend post apprenticeship training.

The description 'Cook' has a double meaning. One can cook in the home. The act of cooking does not qualify a person as a commercial cook. Other exceptions are highly specialist and exclusive cooking occupations,(e.g. a pizza cook) who are cooking but not in the context of working in commercial kitchen with the intention to progress their career to be a chef.

Rank 4
Sous Chef

There are three chefs' ranks with kitchen wide administrative responsibilities. Sous chef, Chef de cuisine and Executive chef. Chefs ranks can be both confusing and contradictory. One can be a Chef de cuisine with two staff, or a Sous chef with 20 staff. The former rank "Chef de cuisine" implies a higher rank, while the latter title "Sous chef" implies a lower rank. The Sous chef role, however, probably demands greater experience and more responsibility.

A Chef who **ENFORCES** and monitors.

Sous chef is the lowest rank with kitchen wide administrative responsibility, their function is principally a second in command and enforcer of the Chef de cuisine policies.

With their position power to enforce the chef's vision as the main point of contact in the day-to-day routine in the kitchen, they additionally carry a huge moral responsibility; they are a mentor, parent, mother, teacher, supervisor and must be a "role model" to trainees.

Additional Sous titles include:

> **Senior sous chef** (indicates that more than one Sous chef operate in the same kitchen spread over two shifts, each allocated to a shift)

> **Executive sous chef** (indicates a second in command who supervises more than one kitchen or property)

There is no such technical position as a junior sous chef, which logically is a misnomer. One is titled a Sous chef, a Senior Sous chef or an Executive sous chef.

REPORTS TO: Chef de cuisine.

| titles - culinary titles and ranks

Typical function and obligatory knowledge:
- Responsible for the coalface operation of the kitchen
- Always includes food preparation

Able to Monitor:
- Budgetary policies
- Hygiene practices
- Food preparation policies
- Food presentation policies
- Legislative Compliance

Must include the ability to:
- Perform the duties of a lesser role
- Proposes potential menu changes
- Technically instruct kitchen staff

RECOMMENDED TO: attend master classes or further education.

Rank 5
Chef de cuisine

A Chef de cuisine title should always include a reference to the name of property. One is not just a Chef de cuisine, one is a Chef de cuisine of xyz hotel or Chef de cuisine of xyz restaurant. This qualifies the responsibility

A Chef who **SUPERVISES** a commercial kitchen.

The Chef de cuisine (Chief of kitchen) is the definitive supervisor of a commercial kitchen. The designation applied irrespective of the size of the brigade (Staff in the Kitchen) or nature of the food service. One may be a Chef de cuisine in a café with a brigade of two or a multinational hotel with a brigade of 32. Their duties vary according to the size of the brigade and usually include food preparation with administrative responsibilities.

Common misnomers include Head chef: The technically correct industry title for a head chef is Chef de cuisine. Otherwise, a silly translation applies "Head of chief of kitchen".

REPORTS TO: Food and beverage manager or immediate administrator.

Typical function and obligatory knowledge:
- Responsible for the complete operation of the kitchen
- Usually includes food preparation

Able to supervise:
- Budget
- Hygiene practices
- Food preparation policies
- Food presentation policies
- Legislative Compliance

Must include the ability to:
- Perform the duties of a lesser role
- Advising senior management on job descriptions
- Allocating human resources within one kitchen
- Allocating physical resources within one kitchen
- Authorise purchase orders
- Implementing new menus
- Interview and select kitchen staff
- Monitor vendors
- Plan menus

RECOMMENDED TO: attend business management courses.

It is worth mentioning here that loyalty is a vital trait required by a Chef de cuisine particularly loyalty to their Sous chef. If a Chef de cuisine has a good Sous chef, guide and teach, but above all, be loyal. If irresponsible, replace with another more deserving Sous chef.

A Chef de cuisine will always find politically correct ways to defend their kitchen brigade from outside the kitchen interference. In the kitchen a good Chef de cuisine will defend their Sous chef in front of others. However, if required the Chef de cuisine will tear the Sous chef apart in private to ensure the misdemeanour will not be repeated.

| titles - culinary titles and ranks

Rank 6
Executive chef

It fails belief the number of Executive chefs actually outnumber the number of establishments with multiple commercial kitchens. To be an "Executive chef", the chef must be responsible for the operation of two or more kitchens, each with their own Chef de cuisines, Sous chefs or chefs. The kitchens may be internally or externally located.

A chef who **MANAGES** a cluster of kitchens.

A chef who is responsible for a single kitchen does not have executive power, therefore is a misnomer to be conferred the titled Executive.

In business terms, executive by definition is the responsibility for a complete organisation, not a unit within an organisation. A Chef de cuisine is the manager of a unit and by being the supervisor of one kitchen has position power. While an Executive chef manages a complete organisation (has external responsibilities with more than one kitchen) therefore executive power.

Mirroring the traditional description for Chef de cuisine, Executive chefs may be responsible for two or 32 units, with the level of their responsibility, additional managerial expertise and industry title identified in their position description.

REPORTS TO: General Manager or administrative equivalent.

Typical function and obligatory expertise:
- Responsible for the operation of multiple kitchens or properties
- Subject to operation may include food preparation

Able to establish and manage:
- Budgets across multiple outlets or cost and profit centres
- Food preparation policies
- Food presentation policies
- Hygiene practices
- Legislative Compliance

Must include the ability to:
- Perform the duties of a lesser role
- Interview and engage senior staff. Negotiate with vendors
- Plan and engineer menus
- Select training programs aimed to develop senior staff
- Set the recipes, methods and styles of food preparation
- Set the style of food presentation
- Sets written policies for cleaning and hygiene practices
- Write job descriptions

RECOMMENDED TO: Attend business management courses.

Newly created culinary positions with non-traditional titles.

Many new culinary titles and career paths exist in the modern culinary industry. Titles such as Director of catering, Research and development chef and more who function outside the traditional role of a kitchen based chef.

A position description and title should identify the scope, duties and responsibilities required to meet the position mission. The equation to determine a culinary rank of a non-traditional title is simply: Responsible for one kitchen equates to Chef de cuisine and for two kitchens equates to Executive chef.

For example: A Chef who is head of a teaching department with multiple training kitchens would rank as Executive chef and a Chef who is head of a teaching department with one teaching kitchen ranks as Chef de cuisine. Professional cookery teachers generally equate to Sous chef (Students report to them and in most cases they directly report to the head).

Corporate Chef, Culinary Director, Food & Beverage Director, Group Chef, Group Executive Chef, Kitchen supervisor, Research and Development Chef and other culinary titles and career paths will be equated with a relative culinary rank irrespective of the extent of the responsibility, as is the case with a Chef de cuisine who can head a brigade of four or 40 cooks and chefs.

Hijacked titles

Celebrity chef is neither a rank nor a culinary role and many times not a cook or chef. A celebrity chef is a media personality who promotes food preparation. Many are not chefs and identified by the way they behave, talk, particularly dress and their need to use a recipe approach to food preparation.

Common sarcastic titles

> **COWBOYS** (see slang page 122)

This unofficial title is applied to anyone who works as a cook, at the same time demonstrate they know very little of the technical process. They muddle through, usually slow and disorderly and flawed in application of techniques. Cowboys also nicknamed a "pretender chef" and identified here because of their substantial numbers in the industry.

Pretender chefs, believe that a chef only needs the ability to place food on a plate to be a chef. The tragedy is that these "pretender chefs" also believe they must be legitimately titled Chef and unfortunately often con the public into believing this as well.

The measurable difference between a chef and a pretender chef is not only the level of their responsibility and skill, but also essentially an intrinsic professional attitude to protect their vocation.

The pretender chef attitude is very much associated with their use of their pseudo title. Because they do not know the real meaning of cook or chef and the responsibilities these ranks inherit, tend to deny the existence of the title cook and view the title as a demeaning status.

Titles that are tributes and acknowledgements

BLACK HAT is not a rank, it is bestowed nationally and globally (Australia - England) and acknowledges a chef's contribution to the development of their local cookery community.

PIONEER is not a rank, it is a national award (Australia - Les Toques Blanches) and acknowledges a chef's contribution to the industry and its inherited cuisine.

MASTER CHEF is not a rank or title; it is an independent industry based qualification, accolade and acknowledgement of the chefs 'SAKE'. A Certified Master Chef is the highest technical achievement possible and can only be a genuine title if based on independent and external examination of a chef's 'SAKE' at the highest level.

Master Chefs must provide evidence of their accrediting organisation against their title or they are pseudo masters. Unfortunately, there are "cowboys" who have never taken external examinations to prove their worth and call themselves Master Chefs.

> *Careful how you treat your brigade their way up the ladder, one day you will meet them on your way down*

10.

for goodness'
SAKE,
self - inflicted
issues

The unrestricted availability of fresh foods, higher educated client expectations, greater disposable incomes, communication, culture, eating habits, education, immigration, media, preservation, social change, technology, and more, has impacted on and changed the career of a cook or chef.

These changes have also affected every other occupation and endeavour.

These radical changes in society required food service to respond to meet new needs. Cooks and chefs have demonstrated their remarkable resilience, as each generation has stepped up to meet these new challenges and expectations of an ever-changing and more demanding client.

While much of the change in commercial cookery has been for the better, principally in health and well-being, working conditions and freedom of culinary expression, it has not all been progress with many of the problems faced by chefs arising out of self-inflicted abuse of their own destiny.

The next chapters outline many of the major issues that have the potential to tarnish the profession.

Explore them, agree or disagree, but please do not disregard. It is your future and no one else's.

> *Just working like a chef one is not good enough, if you start thinking like one you will almost certainly become one*

11. training

for's and againts

formal and

non formal

training

There is growing debate on the relevance of "apprenticeship in cookery" as a training model for a cook. Some believe it is outdated, others have strong opposing views.

An uneasy relationship has always existed between the hospitality industry and education system for training cooks and chefs, possibly inappropriately described as an "apprenticeship in cookery", which suggests the current model may well be the wrong way to train, especially as it leaves the apprentice in between two opposing forces.

Historically an apprentice was someone who legally agreed to work for a specific amount of time in return for instruction in a trade. The training model advanced with the addition of offsite institutional education and an apprenticeship became a partnership between a training provider and a business, with both taking responsibility for the development of the apprentice to become a competent cook.

Excepting group apprenticeship schemes and a handful of large employers, it appears that the number of parties who fully remain committed to their original agreements is getting smaller, so maybe it's time to divorce vocational training from industrial employment and allow the educators to be completely responsible for delivering training of basic culinary skills and knowledge.

The Australian kitchen continues to change, reflecting our multicultural society and taste buds; likewise, the education system is in constant change in an attempt to keep curriculum relevant.

Compounding the historical issues surrounding apprenticeships is the expanding skill shortage in a culturally changing market.

Is an "apprenticeship" a misnomer – or worse, is it downright misleading?

While in the past, there were always industrial issues surrounding apprenticeships, generally the arrangement fulfilled the individual and industry's need for skills; the question now is, does an apprenticeship still fit the future's bill?

training - for's and agaisnts formal and non formal training

The idea that novices learn the trade and day-to-day conventions of a working life while earning a salary is, on the surface, an enormously attractive feature. However, is this really happening?

There is growing evidence that an apprenticeship as a strategy to train future chefs may not be as relevant as it used to be, for example:

> Many employers complain that the system is not delivering appropriate and relevant training because the curriculum is inappropriate and outdated, in spite of the fact that educators have constantly updated curriculum, with changes that have been driven and endorsed by industry representatives.

> Many employers are employing apprentices to take advantage of government incentives primarily to reduce their wages bill.

> The narrow exposure to skills in a market focused on creativity and individuality with many chefs fashioning their own versions of the way food is prepared, presented and served.

> Educators are frustrated to see their basic skills training not reinforced in the workplace, particularly in an occupation where practice makes perfect to achieve industry viable speeds.

> The downsizing of kitchens and brigades, many with unqualified staff, operating with narrow menus and corporate goals that put profit first, naturally inhibit quality on-the-job training.

> The training and supervision of first and second year apprentices is often delegated to older apprentices who would not have adequate experience in supervising and training and should not be the ones doing the teaching.

> Many kitchens run by semi-qualified students or unqualified cooks and chefs lead to bad technical practices.

> Educators are expert at training and assessment and require the time to develop the persons skills, while the employer's mission is to deliver a service or product and make a profit in a time constrained environment; there is a natural conflict between the two missions.

> Government have thrown money over many years to keep apprenticeships in cookery alive and attempt to increase participation, yet completion numbers still decline and attrition is just as bad as ever.

- Young people are now in general more street savvy and do not need the protection that was once afforded by an apprenticeship. Added, social protections and legalisation exist to deal with any inappropriate situations that attempt to take advantage of the naïve.
- Many training providers have live in-house training facilities with functional kitchens and public restaurants, so we in fact have a doubling up of practical training environments, at work and at school.
- Why would an employer want to employ a fully qualified cook when monetary incentives is available to employ an apprentice.
- The notion that apprenticeships increase employment opportunities does not hold up. Employers employ on a needs-basis, not from a social consciousness platform.

These basic arguments indicate that an apprenticeship in cookery is possibly outdated, if not at best contradictory to industry needs.

The better educated, technologically capable generation Y may view an apprenticeship as a second class career path aimed at second-rate achievers, an opinion that is reinforced by programs that openly target underachievers.

However adversely.

There are many benefits in the contemporary "apprenticeship" training system. Commercial cookery, particularly in Australia, has become globalised and multicultural. Kitchens and menus have increasingly developed to be individualistic and many chefs are fashioning their own versions of the way food is prepared, presented and served.

In an industry-wide context, to be a capable mobile cook, it is increasingly necessary to develop skills that are more complex. The irony is, apprentices in a modern kitchen are exposed to a narrower skill set unique to their environment, consequently need to regularly change employers during their formative years to become proficient.

training - for's and agaisnts formal and non formal training

The strength of a modern apprenticeship in cookery is, at the very least, that an apprentice learns the day-to-day conventions of a working life while earning a salary. So what are the dangers of changing the current apprenticeship system to full-time training prior to commencing a working life?

- *Governments invest in training to support and encourage an industry to train its artisans. Changing the apprenticeship system to full- time education prior to full-time employment could hold back government investment in the development of skills that are fundamentally necessary for business creation and growth.*
- *If we completely remove the industry responsibility to train its workforce, why should government continue to invest in training? As a result, the responsibility to invest in training would fall on individual teaching institutes who would be forced to develop their own curriculum and charge appropriate fees.*
- *We would cultivate a disjointed approach to curriculum development and delivery. Subsequently the quality of a cookery course will be totally fee driven. The rich will be able to afford to attend the more expensive institutes while the less fortunate will only be able to attend the cheaper courses.*
- *What happens to institutes especially in the smaller country communities that do not have economies of scale and forced to close down? How then will a passionate young person obtain appropriate training.*
- *Fee-driven institutions in turn will become more profit-focused, which will almost certainly result in an unmanageable downward spiral in the quality of training resulting from pressures to reduce delivery costs.*
- *Notwithstanding many critics of TAFE cookery training, the training of Australian cooks has a proven excellent record and reputation based on achievements of Australian trained cooks and chefs abroad.*
- *The only way to maintain consistency and quality that is vital to support a substantial Tourism and Hospitality industry in Australia is to ensure a centrally driven training system with common curriculum.*

- Full-time pre-employment qualification to enter the industry could further discourage young people to enter cookery. The prospect of having to go to school to obtain a qualification as a cook prior to obtaining a job may well limit demand to a very few highly focused individuals who can afford the training. It appears currently difficult enough to persuade young people to become cooks and the situation would become impossible without the implied security that is inbuilt into an apprenticeship.
- Employers will be likely to favour more mature workers and disadvantage the young by limiting the opportunity to acquire a job and experience. Without an apprenticeship scheme a catch-22 arises: One cannot obtain a job as a cook because of lack of real industry cookery experience and one cannot get the experience because jobs are not available at that age.

There are many obvious inconsistencies and inadequacies with the current apprenticeship training system, notwithstanding the inadequacies "it is better the devil one knows". Provided managers and chefs become far more aware of the fundamentals in a competency- training program and their responsibility in the training model, a modern apprenticeship can work.

The main concerns with the current system voiced by many in the industry is the constant reduction of training hours and resources required to train properly, which has the potential to devalue a cookery qualification.

To become a cook or chef takes time, practice, and more practice, patience and further education and a deal of intelligence. The unfortunate perception by some education administrators and supported by some industry quarters that anyone who has been unable to achieve normal social and educational development or is a social misfit is suitable to train as a cook need reminding that:

> You can take any dummy off the street and attempt to train them as a cook in six weeks, and what is achieved?
> A few may become trained dummies!
> **MOST REMAIN DUMMIES.**
> While many ask why there is a shortage of trained cooks?

12. associations

how professional
is
professional

By most measurements, food quality, training, value, general competencies suggests Australia has one of the most developed and sophisticated commercial cookery industry sectors in the world and in some aspects we lead the way in the culinary arts.

Supporting the many impressive cookery artisans who are shaping Australia as a great culinary destination there are three major chef's associations who target apprentices, cooks and chefs as members. Each have a different mission in the industry and collaborate for the benefit of their members who often belong to multiple organisations.

They run competitions, facilitate networking, offer workshops, organise social events, disseminate information through websites and newsletters, and arrange many other activities that one would expect from a professional association. They provide an immense service to the chef fraternity; particularly given they are operated by honorary committees.

They are professional in the context of representing people who make a living in commercial cookery and they operate professionally in the context of conducting the affairs of the association in a skilful and ethical way.

However, are they representative of commercial cookery as a profession in the context of an occupation where associates are required to meet and maintain common standards?

Further, do they actively promote the advancement of commercial cookery to evolve into a legitimate professional discipline?

Associations that service the needs and promote a profession should:

- *Arrange social and learning activities.*
- *Further the interest of its members.*
- *Have documented codes of practice.*
- *Require proof of minimum technical standards for association.*
- *Require proof of continuous development of members.*

associations - how professional is professional

Notwithstanding the good intentions of existing associations, they lack one if not two of the most important elements to make them a true professional organisation. They do not require applicant members to document their foundation training and development, nor do they request evidence of continuous development during a set period of association for subsequent approval.

Currently the minimum qualification to join a chef's organisation in Australia amounts to the ability to complete an application form, pay a fee, and hope that no one in the organisation questions the application. The process usually involves a cursory committee discussion based around "who know this applicant" followed by an inevitable stamp of approval and consequent lifelong endorsement.

It is time that chef's associations introduced rules requiring prospective members to undergo examinations or demonstrate minimum documented qualifications, subsequently association licence or certify them. Not to mention setting fixed membership terms, at the end of which proof of continuous development is required. If associations claim they represent a "profession" why not go down this path, and review admission prerequisites?

If commercial cookery is ever going to develop into a bona fide profession in every aspect and not continue to be just a job identified by the now meaningless term "chef" (as understood by the public to mean anyone who can follow a recipe) — chef's organisations must consider the difficult but evolutionary road necessary to protect the future by requiring members to justify their association in a more measured, objective way.

Obviously some who may not like the idea of being tested to prove their competence through official documentation or examination will view the change as a threatening move.

This may apply particularly to those who wish to hide behind the term 'chef', because they believe it has some professional connotations for a respected artisan.

Chef's organisations in Australia need to explore this challenging and politically difficult move to create minimum standards of association. By doing so they will demonstrate to the public that professionals in the commercial cookery community will not tolerate amateurs damaging the industry.

It is more than probable that members, who will be lost in such a move, will be replaced by the larger percentage of chefs who do not currently belong to any association and probably do not see the need because there is no chef's organisation in Australia that demands and enforces entry levels, and evidence of continued professional growth.

If ever a public licence is required to be a chef, **it must start at rank and file**, only when professional chef's organisations demonstrate the ability to professionally regulate their members will there be a remote potential to create a public licence to operate as a chef, but this may be dreaming.

This scenario as a phenomena in Australia may well be true of other countries.

**IMPOSSIBLE!
IS ONLY A WORD THAT WAS CREATED BY A
NEGATIVE THINKER.**

13. competitions

it is time

to

remove

the mystery

A Salon Culinaire is a professional cookery competition that normally includes practical and display-based categories, with medals and certificates awarded to successful competitors. Today these categories are often called 'classes' and prize money is usually offered to the winners of the top class.

Salon culinaires are conducted for a number of reasons:
- To test cookery expertise
- Motivate contestants to improve their skills
- Showcase current trends in food preparation
- Promote sponsors' products or services

Skills development is arguably the major objective of a salon culinaire and this is often reflected in the competition design, with various classes testing skills valued by the local cookery community.

While a large number of classes may be available to contestants (canapés, carvings, chocolate classes, gâteau, hot served cold, petits fours, restaurant plates, showpieces etc) there is usually one class that is considered to be the premier event, and which normally mirrors current eating styles or fashion.

This is typically a **HOT KITCHEN** competition and for the past decade the most popular format has been the mystery box, sometimes called the black box.

But is this the right approach for the future?

Reviewing the guides and schedules of chef competitions over many years teaches us a great deal.

Unsurprisingly, competitions with similar influence and location tend to follow a pattern, and over the past 60 years five distinct competition 'phases' have emerged.

During 1950 to 1970 (and earlier), the general format of culinary classes reflected the dwindling classical foodservice era. For example, premier classes in a salon culinaire in 1960 would require a competitor to produce and present a classical eight cover Charlotte Royal or a Chaud-froid decorated leg ham.

competitions - it is time to remove the mystery

In the early 1970s the emphasis shifted to "pièces montées" or "show pieces". These were elaborate constructions used as centrepieces – subsequently ice, butter sculpture, pastillage, salt and cube sugar models became very popular sections. The popularity of showpieces in competition mirrored the fashionable buffet style of meal presentation and service and the kind of artistic skills required in the marketplace.

In the early 1980s, a good example of the way competition profiles matched industry needs was the "Champion State of Australia". A competition that required teams of chefs from across the country to present hot served cold, showpieces, hot kitchen and sweets buffet which were identical to the participation requirements for the Culinary Olympics and encouraged participation as a training ground for chefs who wished to represent Australia overseas.

In early 1990 the popular hot-served cold dishes and hot kitchen classes took the premier class position (restaurant plates, three course dinner menu, Menu Gastronomique, etc) emphasising both the trend away from the display buffet/smorgasbord and the move toward small fine dining restaurants where food on the plate became the focus.

Since the late 1990s, the "mystery box" has accentuated the creativity and individuality of the current generation of chefs who increasingly have their own ideas about how food should be prepared, presented, and served. In a mystery box, all main ingredients (principally the proteins) are confidential until the commencement, thereby testing the creativity of the contestant.

However, change is always with us, in 2014 where the contemporary chef needs to be extremely well-planned and more resource-smart, efficient and consistent than ever before.

Chefs today do not create dishes or menus in their daily routine; they carefully plan, cost, rehearse, and review their concept dish before placing the refined version on the menu.

If these are the most valuable skills possessed by chefs today, we need to test them in the premier classes of salon culinaires especially now that careful planning has trumped creativity, it is time to remove all mystery and inform contestants exactly what to expect in any hot kitchen class.

By removing the mystery component, we will undoubtedly achieve better-planned and practiced results. This change will also be a win for sponsors who will reap the benefits of controlled innovation and more thoughtful use of their products.

Removing the mystery should also eliminate the many disastrous entries from chefs who blindly experiment in a public arena with products they have not used before, which embarrasses the sponsors.

A major national competition held in 2011 and again in 2012 provided evidence in support of this argument. Two separate classes were offered, one for senior chefs who were given a mystery box of proteins and another for apprentices, which were identical except the apprentices were informed about the proteins months in advance.

The overall result was conclusive: while both seniors and trainees displayed innovation, the apprentice class consistently produced meals at a much higher standard. We still had a winner and all the standard assessments applied.

The mystery box class in cookery competitions has had its day and it is time to remove the secrecy in hot kitchen competitions.

It is time to put creativity on the backburner and bring back some sensible R&D into the competitive arena; we do not need to continue encouraging creativity, inventiveness is here to stay.

| competitions - it is time to remove the mystery

Culinary competitions and sponsored programs that advertise for apprentice chefs should accurately promote that they seek apprentice cooks.

These programs are highly respected by chefs; they provide an enormous benefit to the industry and the apprentices who are fortunate to participate. However, they surely aim to develop future chefs and culinary leader's. They truthfully should advertise for the best of the best trainees or apprentice cooks who aspire to be a chef, not for chefs who aspire to be a chef.

The International Exhibition of Culinary Art commonly referred to as the Culinary Olympics conducted in Germany every four years is the premier global Salon Culinaire. The competition attracts chefs from over 50 nations and thousands of individual chefs who aim to show their culinary skills. Winning a gold medal at this event is the epitome of culinary competition achievement.

14. uniform

do chefs

understand

branding?

Most uniforms have a purpose, worn to distinguish an occupation or standardise the image of a unique group in society and in some cases for safety or hygiene.

A uniform is a symbolic representation of its group, it is a brand, and even its individual parts and features exist for a reason. The more easily identified the brand, usually the more interesting its historical significance.

This is very true of a traditional cook's uniform, a uniform steeped in history that has in part stood the test of time, through industrial and cultural changes, fashions, wars, and for hundreds of years, till now.

The traditional cook's uniform currently found in commercial kitchens across the globe, particularly in Western commercial kitchens, instantly identifies the unique vocation of a commercial cook.

Originally derived as a political statement, the legend of a cook's uniform is believed to have originally emerged after the fall of the Byzantine Empire nearly six hundred years ago when the imperial chefs sought refuge in monasteries and adopted the habits of the monks.

During that era the chefs *(in all probability, egotistically characteristic and attempting to be different)* also decided that their clothes should look different from those worn by the real monks and abbots and wore grey. Today the only remaining symbol of the original habit is the hat, which is a representation of the Bishops' Mitre.

Chefs who historically influenced the current uniform include Marie-Antoine Carême acknowledged as the developer of the current cook's jacket who remodelled the attire to white in the mid-19th century, as he believed it was more hygienically appropriate in a kitchen.

In addition, August Escoffier, the accepted king of chefs and father of the modern day kitchen who also believed the cleanliness of the cook's uniform was very important, and that it promoted professionalism, further influenced its current design.

uniform - do chefs understand branding

The cook's uniform in one fashion or another, has existed for hundreds of years and has evolved over time to traditionally consist in parts of a reversible double breasted long sleeved jacket that shields the body from heat of appliances while protecting the body against burns from hot splashes. A white apron that likewise is a hygienic and safety garment, light check pants, a necktie and the white toque, form the rest of the uniform.

The most imposing and distinguishing part of a cooks uniform is the toque or hat with its characteristic legendary pleats that supposedly represent the ways a cook can cook an egg. **It is the brand of a chef.**

> ### ➤ DEBATABLE INCONSISTENCY:
> *How valid is a chef's hat award for a restaurant to acknowledge the quality of their food when the chef is not willing to wear the symbol?*

> *The classic iconic torque is not only a head covering, more importantly it is a globally acknowledged symbol of a trained cook worn by professionals who are proud of their trade.*

> *Chefs who wear striped blue instead of pure white aprons should realise the striped apron was originally a part of butchers' uniform and the stripes designed to camouflage the splashes of blood from handling raw meat.*
> *A striped blue apron is not as clear a signal of hygiene as pure white is, it does not visibly demonstrate a sparkling clean appearance and can subconsciously place doubt about hygiene in the eyes of the client.*

Today the neckerchief is symbolic and used for aesthetic purposes only, principally worn in competitions, at official chef's events or mainly in the kitchen by traditionalist chefs to give the uniforms a more traditional look.

Cooks and Chefs in some properties in Australia have replaced the toque with a cap, said mainly for reasons of comfort. Unfortunately a head covering is not worn at all by some pretentious cooks or chefs.

The concern with the change in not wearing a toque is one of **branding the vocation.**

In days gone by approaching a gate where VIPs, no matter who, had their credentials checked by security, only to have the security guard allow a chef (a total stranger) to enter without a pass as they said "hi Chef", only because of a simple toque. Such is the symbolic power of a traditional chef's hat.

The symbolic hat enjoys global respect, it is not gender, race, political, or religion aligned; has historical significance and is an established brand of an occupation. Yet the inconsistency that some chefs show when they demand and rightfully expect total loyalty from their staff while being disloyal to their vocation and colleagues is puzzling.

Why do some chefs, who by all other measurements are professional, not promote their vocation in public by wearing a globally recognised traditional symbol of a trained artisan in public?

There is a visual contradiction in terms when chefs of an organisation that uses the icon in its name, has chefs who do not wear a torque and, do not brand their association?

This indiscretion is understandable of celebrity chefs who are not real cooks or chefs, who are not trained or educated to know different.

There is reasonable evidence that wearing a cap as an alternative in a commercial kitchen is a comfortable, safe, and hygienic garment for everyday use, and is both contemporary and appropriate.

| uniform - do chefs understand branding

HOWEVER...

It is bizarre that Executive Chefs, Chef de cuisines, Heads of schools, or others who are supposedly leaders and who will gain the most from associating with the image; allow their apprentices, or cookery staff to walk through a hotel foyer, serve behind a buffet or attend a practical class without a traditional cook's hat, is unfortunately all too common.

It is amateurish for a cook or chef to appear on TV, in a magazine or in a newspaper while cooking on a stove in a kitchen without a symbolic traditional hat. They let themselves and all their colleagues down and degrade the whole cookery industry. They literally miss the opportunity to maintain the strength and image that brands their vocation and, unfortunately, many do not realise the damage they do to the industry in their quest to be cool.

This phenomenon is primarily an Australian experience. Overseas cooks and chefs, cookery staff on cruise ships, many multi national hotels and renowned restaurants still promote the brand with many Chef de cuisines insisting on the standard. The indiscretion appears to emerge mainly in trendy restaurants with cooks and chefs who are not yet fully mature or possibly embarrassed they may be recognised as a cook or a chef.

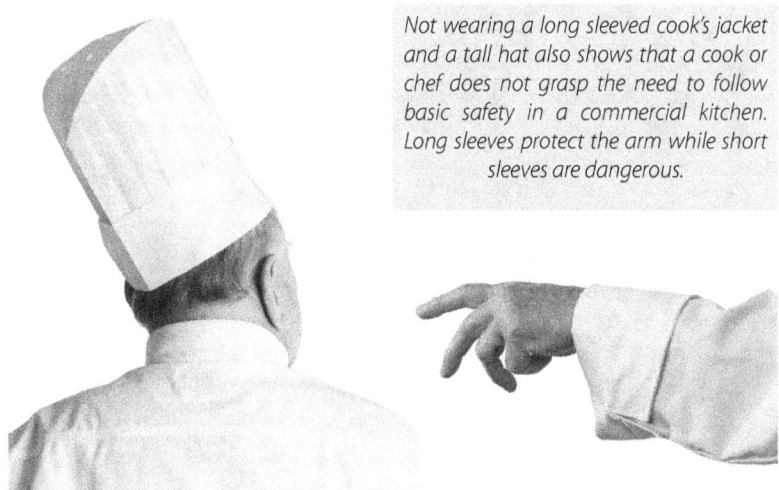

Not wearing a long sleeved cook's jacket and a tall hat also shows that a cook or chef does not grasp the need to follow basic safety in a commercial kitchen. Long sleeves protect the arm while short sleeves are dangerous.

15. bully beef

is being a bully,

a chef's natural

temperament?

History tends to portray the typical cook / chef as a loud-mouthed bully unable to prudently hold liquor, uses colourful language, is hot-tempered and works in a hot kitchen.

Understaffed and working with a semi-trained potpourri of employees from diverse ethnic origins, they drive their bodies and brains on a daily basis to levels few other professions would accept.

Through all this, they endeavour to achieve budget targets sometimes set by ill-informed and incompetent managers or accountants who have very little idea of the constant pressure and time constraints in the day-to-day operation of a commercial kitchen.

In the name of an addiction commonly called 'passion', the hard-working cook / chef attempts to satisfy a voracious dining public who are convinced they know more about the preparation, presentation, and service required of the dishes on the menu than does the trained professional who has slaved to indulge their fantasies.

But do these stressful and occasionally deplorable physical and emotional working conditions make it acceptable or excusable for chefs to bully and abuse their staff?

The irresponsible bullying or abuse of staff is not acceptable in any circumstance, irrespective of the working conditions. Apart from the legal obligations that justifiably protect the rights of staff in the commercial kitchen, there is more than just the legal perspective.

Having enjoyed a career that has involved just about every style and level of responsibility a chef can achieve I fortunately discoverd very early in my career that managing a commercial kitchen is all about motivation, and definitely not intimidation. Furthermore in the latter part of my career assuming associated roles with direct links to professional cookery, I have seen and experienced just about every workplace scenario imaginable.

Having had the privilege of working with many accomplished chefs who were superb with their food philosophy and skills on the plate and great kitchen leaders, I find that the ones who really stood

bully beef - is being a bully, a chef's natural temperament

out from the crowd were not ill-tempered, nor did they browbeat their staff, despite having to work physically and mentally hard in a demanding environment.

In addition to being gifted cooks, they were smart enough to realise that they needed to surround themselves with a great kitchen team and treat their brigade with dignity.

Calmly, clearly and with propriety they would seek to develop the skills of their team. Whether it was an apprentice cook or sous chef, these leaders helped and encouraged them to perform at a high level and regularly exceed the expectations of their role.

They built a team that operated on mutual trust, respect and loyalty. The kitchen brigade, who admired, supported, protected and even went to substantial lengths to defend their leader at every opportunity enhanced their reputation. This was loyalty, which worked from the top down and in both directions, born from mutual respect.

Every era has its challenges, as did hot steamy environments of yesteryear. Since significant changes in working conditions have evolved, the modern chef does not work in conditions that engender appalling behaviour.

Commercial kitchens have air-conditioners, evaporative coolers, extractors, safety equipment, lighting and numerous other appliances making the contemporary working environment a safe and healthy one. Improved working hours, sophisticated communication and realistic expectations by many competent managers and better-educated employees now encourage a team spirit and a reasonable and pleasurable work environment.

As such, there are absolutely no physical or emotional grounds for bullying in a modern kitchen. Commercial kitchens no longer have the culture or physical conditions that condone violence or abuse, and if a supervisor or the chef is a bully, it is time they left the industry and took their *"attitude"* somewhere else.

There can be many reasons for inappropriate behaviour in a kitchen. Bullying or aggressive behaviour, and to a lesser extent swearing, are usually pointers to the chef being uneducated, insecure, or a sufferer of depression. It is time that chefs in small or large kitchens who lack fundamental leadership skills and bully staff are retrained.

Chefs' associations in Australia endorse a common moral code of conduct for cooks and chefs and must take their obligations seriously and enforce them. In our advanced professional environment, we should not operate within only a minimum legal framework.

The word professional has two interrelated connotations; one is a trained person who earns a living in a specialised discipline, and that definition is inseparably linked to a person who manages their own standards within agreed boundaries.

> *Never has the reality been clearer —*
> *if a chef cannot tolerate the heat,*
> *get out of the kitchen.*

CHEFS, IT IS NOT AS HOT AS IT USED TO BE

16. media

when it comes to TV, everybody's tastes are different

Celebrity chefs on television reality and other shows who use offensive language and publicly abusing people are abhorrent for basic reasons.

While everyone has the right to their own opinion, freedom of speech is important and every adult has the right to watch what they wish, these unprofessional actors personally insult real chefs by their actions.

When celebrity chefs portray chefs as incapable of expressing themselves without the use of profanities and unable to coach staff without appalling abuse, genuine chefs and all commercial kitchens have the potential to be considered by the public as "guilty by association" and consequently painted by the same brush.

It is simple reality that a great deal of the general public are gullible enough to believe that these shows depict the norm for a commercial kitchen and they demonstrate the customary "character" for a chef.

Because there are fundamentals here, people swear only when they have not mastered the ability to express themselves in the use of the English language and supervisors who abuse their staff in public show they are not experienced in people management.

Chefs are as much "change agents", or in the business of motivating, teaching, and developing their staff just as any other responsible manager of people. Any responsible and educated manager or chef realise that they do not need to use foul language or socially unacceptable abuse to obtain a desired result.

Commercial kitchens, like any other environment, occasionally get "hot" and irregular swear words are used and more than necessary abused. Just as doctors, nurses, ambulance officers, and even teachers are guilty of this "steam". However, it is also a matter of self-discipline, maturity and learning to appreciate that such behaviour is not appropriate in certain places, especially in public, or particularly when you are representing an industry.

Chefs do not go out in front of clients and swear at them, nor would

| media - when it comes to tv, everybody's tastes are different

a professional accept profanities and abuse in a teaching institute because their kitchens supposedly are models of "high stressed environments".

Educated chefs learn to control themselves; they become skilled at controlling their temper, particularly in times of crisis, which we all know can happen in a kitchen.

Younger chefs do not also realise that it also took dedicated and passionate teachers and industry chefs over the past 20 – 30 years to convince the public to change their perceptions of chefs and accept that the vocation is a decent and professional one.

Literally, we have gone through "eras of attitudes". In earlier days when a boy told his parents that he wished to become a "cook" there was a good chance that he was painted as the "poof in the family".

Additionally, the community generally was prejudiced against females in a commercial kitchen, as they were considered incapable of surviving the pressures and anyway incompetent as cooks, let alone a "female leader" with their own kitchen, impossible!

Another perception was the era, where the public believed that chefs were constantly intoxicated and always had a "fag" in the corner of their mouth.

These myths have gradually been addressed by professional cookery teachers and industry chefs and shown not to be true and these unfortunate perceptions have been fundamentally eradicated. Let us not regress and create a perception that a chef cannot speak decently and lead a kitchen without abusive mannerisms. Fundamentally, a celebrity chef who swears and unacceptably abuses people in the public arena is guilty of taking the industry backwards.

It could be just another reason why young people are not entering a commercial cookery career. What parent in their right mind would want their child to join the cookery industry having seen programs that illustrate a chef as an appalling supervisor?

What intelligent young person would want to work in conditions where they will experience abuse in front of others?

What bad messages do these shows send out to the public about the cookery industry and the ability of chefs to responsibly deal with people?

Worse still, will this behaviour on television blatantly encourage the wrong personality to join the cookery industry, particularly those who see themselves as bullies?

17. spelling

should that

windyloo

be

vindaloo?

Chef talk, culinary terminology and colloquialisms are powerful, often underestimated tools in the daily operation of a commercial kitchen, even every-day conversation and written communication is essential to the smooth operation of any kitchen.

Unfortunately, neither written nor verbal communication is in the skill set of the average chef who has to use both daily to communicate to clients and staff. Moreover, this deficiency is becoming increasingly obvious to the public in menu writing.

Ordinary language - culinary terms, punctuation, grammar, all that stuff we were fortunate enough to have been taught in school or culinary college is a skill required on a daily basis by chefs.

Chefs write memos, reports, issue instructions and most importantly are responsible for the main image of their foodservice: **THE MENU**.

All too often we see commas, apostrophe's, capital letters and bold appear out of context or missing foreign punctuation (predominately French). But there is far, far worse, we also find the incorrect use of technical terms, read embarrassing spelling errors and come across the ultimate embarrassment, the use of downright stupid descriptions.

Have menus got to a point where, if by chance dishes are spelt and described accurately, instead of being the expected norm, the menu stands out as extraordinary.

Further, chefs often attempt to be creative with their menu descriptions, purely under the misapprehension that if a dish is euphemistically described it will magically change into something wonderful.

A GOOD MENU IS ACCURATE, TRUTHFUL, EASILY UNDERSTOOD AND AVOID OVERZEALOUS DESCRIPTIONS

spelling - should that windyloo be vindaloo

Examples of ***incorrect*** use of technical terms:

BALLONTINE	Indicates a boned and rolled leg of poultry, often incorrectly applied to describe any roll of meat.
CANAPÉS	Refers to bite-sized, often presented more like an open sandwich.
CARPACCIO	A name once given to raw thinly sliced beef, anything can now be incorrectly a thin sliced anything.
CASSOULET	Real Cassoulet should have small white beans in it, it often has any kind of beans.
CHIFFONADE	Of carrot? Disregarding that a Chiffonade should only be cut from a green leaf.
TOMATO CONCASSÉ	Or technically skinned and deseeded fresh tomato flesh, is replaced by crushed tinned or minced tomatoes.
CONFIT	The name given to a process of preserving and slow cooking protein in fat, which is now often used to refer to just about anything cooked in anything for a long time.
JULIENNE	Technically meaning cut like straw, often presented like batons.
TAPAS	Is now anything but small and disregards it is served with a drink.
TARTE TATIN	Should be a classical caramelised apple tart, now found as a combination of pastry and thinly sliced fruit or even vegetables.

Every professional industry has its own set of terms and expressions, essentially to standardise practice and educate the client, cookery included. The accurate application of technical terminology is essential for any respected discipline.

Chefs must understand the culinary terminology is a resource and reference; terms represent a global agreement by chefs on a set of methods and techniques.

> Technical terms represent an industry standard and educate the public

> A misspelled word can destroy a beautiful dish

Additionally there are the appalling spelling errors that add insult to inaccurate descriptions:

- ✗ Ragout served in a shaving dish.
- ✗ Roast beef served with Dejohn mustard.
- ✗ Our special sweet today is Chocolate Mouse.
- ✗ The steak is accompanied by Sharon sauce made from béarnaise sauce with tomato.
- ✗ Frish cakes with chips. Wonder if they were also fresh and served flied ships.
- ✗ Open sandwitch. Must be a magic sandwich.
- ✗ Hand and cheese. This indicates the guard on the slicer was not used.
- ✗ Chicken Gordon blue. A blue ribbon example of carelessness.
- ✗ Vietnamese Spring Rool.
  A 'revolutionary" way of making a roll.
- ✗ Killpatrick. This would have to be murdered .

DO NOT LAUGH THESE ARE REAL!

No matter how good a cook is, correct spelling is a way of thinking and reflects directly on the chef. An error on a menu gives the client one of their very first impressions of the foodservice and **first impressions count.**

| spelling - should that windyloo be vindaloo

Additionally some chefs believe outlandish creativity is achieved using meaningless or unnecessary descriptions:

Duck shanks	Ocean caught fillets of fish
Freshly skinned	Roast Maryland
Ice-cold salad	Twice cooked

KISS means: Keep It Simple Stupid!

Another issue involves the growing tendency to see the hijacking of culinary terms by manufacturers who twist their meaning to portray something that they are not. Unfortunately, they do not see, nor understand the historical significance, of culinary heritage or the need to respect the universal language used in professional cookery.

When something is identified wrongly in the media, on a menu, in a shop, or on a supermarket shelf on a packet, the incorrect becomes the "norm" as the unknowing and confused general public accept the incorrect as correct. An example of this is a sirloin of lamb openly sold in supermarkets. Sirloin of lamb, "Sirloin" owes its name to King Charles 11 who knighted the joint of beef; subsequently sirloin is accurate only in the context of beef. Yet back strap of lamb has been renamed sirloin of lamb. This blatantly disregards the culinary heritage behind the original name of Sirloin.

Then there is the example of spatchcock. Spatchcock is a way of preparing a young chicken and should technically not be used as a name for a product. It is a spitchcocked chicken, not a spitchcocked spatchcock.

These are small examples of bastardisation of the industry language that is diminishing the history that underpins commercial cookery.

Whose fault, I suggest the uneducated manager who takes the word of an incompetent chef leading to a scenario where the blind leads the blind all because someone is promoted to the level of his or her incompetence.

Artistic licence is good, and no one wishes to return to the rigidity of yesteryear, however it is vital that any description of a product or process maintains and recognises the important value of culinary heritage.

Training ensures efficiency, uniform brands a discipline, codes of practice reinforce attitudes, terminology standardise practice. Added accurate descriptions leads to industry reliability and consistency, moreover public confidence.

> *Look for examples and you will find a potential cancer of growing abuse of technical terminology. Strongly object to misuse of culinary heritage and guard culinary traditions.*

18. allergies

who is

responsible?

the chef

or

the client?

In 2008, during the black Saturday bushfire crisis, I volunteered to deliver meals to a local community centre set up to feed a few hundred fire fighters coming in shifts and all in need of something nourishing. The situation looked grim across Victoria and everyone was trying to assist in any way possible.

To respond to the emergency, the food had been hastily prepared but safely produced, quickly cooled and vacuum-packed early in the morning. Its temperature was carefully checked and dated as we packed the individual sealed bags filled with pasta and bolognaise sauce. As a precaution, ice was added to keep the food at a safe temperature during the 1.5 hours journey from the college preparation kitchen to the community emergency centre set up to feed hundreds of volunteer fire fighters.

Arriving with my precious cargo in tightly sealed commercial-sized esky containers, I was confronted by an environmental health surveyor. Aware that the food had been responsibly handled and safely transported, I was confident that it would pass any inspection.

First, out came the thermometer and, as expected, food temperatures were well within acceptable limits.

Eager and ready to unload, I was then informed that the delivery could not be accepted because *"there wasn't a nutritional information label on the packages and some people may be allergic to their contents"*.

There are times in one's career when screaming and profane expressions that fit a situation seem totally inadequate. But keeping my cool (which climatically on the day was not easy), I explained the urgency of the situation and that we would advise the people who were serving of the basic ingredients as a precaution in the event that anyone asked.

The decision appeared literally touch and go as we increased the level of our discussions, until finally commonsense prevailed. But this was only after we debated the likelihood that anyone with an allergy would naturally inquire about the content of the meal, that

allergies - who is responsible, the chef or the client

the servers would be made aware of the basic ingredients, that a label on the packet would not be seen by the consumer anyway and I had made assurances that the next delivery would contain a nutritional information label on each packet.

Instead of respecting his knowledge and understanding his role in the crisis (he had simply to say "please inform servers of the ingredients so that anyone who asks can be made aware of any potential issue") I conversely left the scene with nothing but contempt for his power-hungry attitude and attempt to justify his existence in a situation that called for sensible flexibility and reasonable rationale.

This event more than any other made me aware that chefs cannot be responsible for others who have an allergy problem and that individuals must take responsibility for their own wellbeing, crisis or not.

Obviously chefs and the restaurant staff need to be aware that certain foods or their by-products can cause an allergic reaction in some people. Research shows that 90 per cent of allergic reactions occur from the following foods and in rare cases these allergic reactions can be extremely severe and even life-threatening: *cereals containing gluten, shellfish and their products, egg and egg products, fish and fish products, milk and milk products, peanuts and other nuts such as almonds, cashews, walnuts, Soybeans, and their products.*

Of course chefs need to be aware of the basic ingredients in their dishes and the potential dangers of allergies caused by them. However it has to be the diner who must take primary responsibility for their own personal circumstances and wellbeing by informing the wait staff about their allergies, particularly when ordering, and should enquire if a dish contains a potentially harmful ingredient.

Obviously also there is some collective responsibility. The wait staff must take food allergy comments seriously and should never guess the ingredients of a dish or dismiss the comment as trivia. They must check with the chef. Just as the idiom **"When in doubt throw it out"** applies to food storage, in food allergies "a wise chef will always be cautious" and, if in doubt, always advise a known safe alternative.

The short descriptive way modern menu items are expressed more than adequately provides the opportunity for chefs to discreetly identify major potentially harmful ingredients.

There is a limit on the allergen information that can be identified on a menu and chefs cannot be expected to specify every ingredient that can potentially cause an allergic reaction. Imagine a menu that requires complete nutritional information:

MENU

"Fresh Garden Salad tossed with French dressing".

Please be aware this salad contains garden greens that have been grown with the following nutrients: mineral salts, gravel mix, nitrogen, potassium, phosphorous, calcium and magnesium. Our extra virgin olive oil contains a triglyceride composition made up of monounsaturated fats, oleic acid and polyunsaturated fats with some traces of tocopherols and polyphenols. Our balsamic vinegar includes glucose and fructose and organic acids: mainly acetic, gluconic, malic, tartaric and succinic acids, and may contain traces of polyphenols. All this is combined by our chefs to give you our house-made basic salad dressing.

19. menu planning

are young guns losing passion?

> *Do you want chips and salad or chips and veggies with your roast madam?*

Show me how passionate you are and I can tell how good a cook or chef you really are. Cooking awakens a monster in a natural cook or chef, an inner force that makes them go beyond the normal, an energy that compels them to stand out and be different.

Just to see a smile or hear a complimentary remark acts like a drug, it ignites or satisfies an inner mysterious desire. Passionate cooks are never lazy, always seeking new experiences, even when cooking simply, they feel alive and just going to work is a joy.

Passion is an uncontrollable driver that never allows a true cook or chef to get comfortable.

Yet, why do we see signs that this fundamental characteristic is declining in some young guns and even in some more mature chefs, notably those in the local eateries?

Becoming lazy is a sign that a chef is losing passion. When they stop wishing to experiment with new dishes, ask where a product came from, keep the same menus because it is too difficult to compile a new one, or stop worrying about client comments, then it is time to reflect, why?

Why, is it almost a certainty to find : Bangers and Mash, Chicken Parmigiana, Hamburgers, Liver and Bacon, Roast, Spaghetti Bolognaise or Steak with Pepper Sauce featured on most local menus when there are literally thousands of alternatives?

A clear example of this trend is the growing tendency to offer fried potato chips with everything.

Potatoes have been a staple menu item for all types of large and small establishments for a long time and the potato has played a significant role on most good menus.

menu planning - are young guns losing passion

Potatoes are steeped in history, at one time, the potato was incorrectly believed to have caused leprosy, the vegetable was at one stage used as a medicine to ward off rheumatism, elevated to the status of being considered an exotic food and there are recipe books written purely on potato preparations.

The humble potato is acknowledged for its taste and nutritive value and has rightfully evolved into a staple that enjoys mass popularity and is considered a principle vegetable in most meals.

It is not many decades ago, prior to the culinary revolution of the nineties, that Australian chefs only served two styles of potato, old and new. And the varieties available to the commercial sector were extremely limited to almost washed and unwashed.

The revolutionary transformation to Australian cuisine over the past 30 years in which chefs creatively adapted many classical potato preparations has been nothing short of astonishing and we experienced superb menus that included a sensible range of creative and ingenious potato accompaniments.

However, has the innovation peaked? Is it because of apathy, availability, diet, cost, demand, skills, knowledge, supply, or maybe simply a declining passion in chefs that we find more and more menus with emphasis on deep fried chips and less of the other basic potato alternatives?

Apart from lumpy watery mashed spuds and "ugly cut chunky roasted something or other", we currently appear to have chips, chips, and more chips.

Unfortunately in many local family restaurants and pubs we routinely experience the "chips and salad or chips and veggies" syndrome irrespective of the method of cookery applied to the main dish.

When did you last enjoy: Anna, Au Four, Boulangère, Croquette, Creamed, Dauphine, Duchesse, Gaufrette, Lyonnaise, Parsley, Parmentier, Sauté, Straw, Soufflé or any one of many other basic dishes that regularly appeared on menus in one form or another.

Where has the gratin, herbed, scalloped, smashed, or many chef's contemporary interpretation of these basic styles using combinations of chilli, garlic, herbs, pesto, salsa, soy, or wasabi as creative points of difference disappeared and why?

- It should not be food cost, as many of the styles yield is equal to or greater than the cost of purchasing and frying chips.
- It is not an issue of availability; chefs have a huge range of varieties available and additionally varieties that better suit a method of preparation.
- It ought not to be labour, as generally it's cheaper to in-house produce many of the potato alternatives than purchase and fry frozen chips.
- It cannot be demand driven as clients choose from the menu.
- Surely, it is not diet, as generally clients are more weight conscious and attempt to avoid fatty fried foods.
- It is not a lack of knowledge; cooks learn potato preparations during training.

The probable fundamental reason unfortunately appears to be that frozen chips are easy to purchase and easy to cook and chefs are being just plain apathetic.

This example represents an unfortunate trend also seen across menus in entrées, mains, and sweets. Not so in high-end food focused restaurants, but in middle casual dining.

What needs to be asked:

- Where has the passion gone?
- Where is the creativity that chefs are known for?
- Why has the analysis in planning a complete balanced meal vanished?
- And where is the real choice for the client?

Restaurants that target clients across the whole spectrum of dining experiences need to keep serving chips for demand purposes, however they should also offer alternatives that will satisfy and educate their clients. **OR, ARE CHEFS JUST BECOMING LAZY ?**

20. food presentation

it is a

question

of era

> *A very broad view of food presentation in the past 50 years described with tongue in cheek.*

Obviously these eras did not apply to every establishment nor did they exactly coincide at the same time. the times are approximate however there was always a "fashion" that usually emanated in a trendy restaurant and spread like an inferno across other kitchens.

Like the "Castillo" fashion. (In the early eighties where Castello cheese almost became a cult), it was found everywhere on menus and presented in many ways.

THE INFLEXIBLE ERA PRE HISTORY

As a backdrop, we start in the 1950 – 1960 era, when food presentation and menu planning was very standardised, formal and rigid.

At the high end of the market in England, the last breath of the classical system struggled to survive against growing pressures from increasing labour costs.

The best food presentation was found in hotels with à la carte restaurants prepared in a classical partie system with an à la carte menu where customers chose their own accompaniments.

Vegetables and starch were presented apart from the protein on silver platters.

Recipes were derived from the classical bible of a Le Repertoire de La Cuisine or Larousse Gastronomic and glistening silver platters left the kitchen carried by formally dressed waiters, some with tailcoats.

No chef would dare to change the way the menu was worded, prepared, presented or served.

Even the local restaurant attempted to reproduce this style as

| food presentation - it is a question of era

much as possible and there was consistency (be it boring) in menu descriptions and style of food presentation.

Basically, the meal was presented with the protein on a silver platter, vegetables and sauce were served apart and waiters would serve to the diner's plate at the table.

In Australia only a very few establishments (mainly in emerging Sydney and Melbourne city properties) were sophisticated enough to attempt to resemblance the European silver service era.

An extremely small pool of skilled chefs, (almost able to be counted on one hand) attempted to replicate the European standard against the insurmountable odds of unskilled kitchen staff and an uneducated client in the new culinary frontier.

THE AWAKENING ERA 1960 - 70

Than came the huge change in food presentation.

The 1956 Olympic games in Melbourne, had a huge impact on foodservice in Australia, especially with the arrival of a number of experienced chefs with a cosmopolitan view of food preparation and presentation.

This kindled the first measurable shift in food presentation across Australia in the 60's. Arguably this shift also emerged from a combined need to reduce labour and material costs, and affected by the changing parti system that amalgamated many traditional parties and additionally, the impact of the growing pool of immigrants who were skilled chefs.

At first generally vegetables, starch and accompaniments all appeared on the plate with the main item. Plates were completed in the kitchen, they were generally flat, arranged like a clock face and usually consisted of five main components:

Protein, Starch, Vegetable, Sauce (napped over the protein) and a Garnish.

Nearly all plates for entrée, main, sweet and side were round and very rarely oval.

Amazingly one could order in different restaurants for example a Tournedos Rossini or a Vienna Schnitzel and the plate appeared almost as if it had come out of the same kitchen plated by the same chef, the only potential difference being a logo on the plate.

There was a mandatory 9PM, 12PM, 3AM and 6AM clock face. The 6 AM position was always the main item on the plate with the other three usually 3 AM the starch, the 12 PM the garnish and the 9 PM the vegetable.

Another significant aspect was the mandatory garnish on every course, be it often just a sprig of parsley. Very few chefs had discovered the everyday use of fresh herbs, basil was the name of a hotel manager in a new program called Faulty Towers and chives, oregano, chervil were known to be types of something dried?

This was still a very inflexible era and chefs generally conservative in nature.

About this time (in the late 60's) radicals began to put sauces under food and napping gradually became *"old fashioned"*. Generally gone, but definitely in their last breath, were the days of salvers with worn gray edges.

This was birth of a new age *"radical"* chef who started the revolution in freedom of menu expression, preparation and presentation.

THE MINUSCULE ERA 1970 – 1975

Slowly boiling in Europe for about 15 years was a cookery movement and philosophy that was not only about to establish a major change to menus, but also shake the very foundation in preparation and presentation across the world.

This chapter arrived in Australia in the early 70's as *"Nouvelle Cuisine"* swept the world. Unfortunately mainly because the new era was not fully understood by many Australian chefs, it evolved into *"children's portions put on a plate by an interior decorator"*.

In that era the main item was centred in the plate surrounded by tiny, tiny items that were so small you felt almost embarrassed to eat them and most went home after a function or dinner to have a meal.

THE SEA CHANGE ERA 1975 – 1985.

Having been driven underground for a decade for fear of persecution by the diminishing classicists and the apostles of Nouvelle Cuisine, the radicals began to reappear on the scene, and in the name of artistic cooking licence all sorts of weird combinations appeared on menus.

About this time a few chefs tried to *"surf and turf"* with fish and chicken Kabobs, lobster quenelles on top of steaks and many more weird seafood and meat combinations.

Also about this time garnishing became a cult, roses were formed from tomato skins, animals and birds carved from carrots, serviettes folded into flowers, gondolas and swans.

Even your author was responsible for really some strange combinations and presentations, like baby cantaloupe cut into swans and used as an entrée. Or serving *"honey with blue cheese"*.

Presentation now also focused on the use of paper. With every plate requiring a doily and every plate requiring an under plate and guess what? The under plate also used a doily.

THE GIGANTIC ERA 1985 – 1990

Having found that no one was actually hung, drawn and quartered, the radicals grew stronger and next change to appear was the extra large plate syndrome.

There is a theory that this was actually a response to Nouvelle Cuisine when chefs started feeling guilty about placing normal size portions of food on a plate and so reacted by enlarging the plate so that the meal had a pseudo "Nouvelle" look.

THE STACKING ERA 1990 – 1995

Chefs then progressed into the stacking era where every item was a "Tian". An edible leaning tower of Pisa.

One would look at the meal towering high on the plate, knowing that layer upon layer of vegetables or greens were stacked on top of a hidden potato galette or such.

This whole new concept I am sure was created to persecute and guarantee nervous breakdowns amongst waiters who required the skills of a Cirque de Soleil act to get the plate to the table.

THE SPRINKLING ERA 1990 – 1995

Not happy with every dish representing a phallic symbol or leaning tower of Pisa , chefs then decided the new presentation style was to sprinkle every plate with something.

This was a real opportune shift as one could also read their future in every plate, "who needed tealeaves in a cup to see their future".

Main course plates were liberally sprinkled with herbs, and sweets dusted with sugar right off the edge of the plate.

Most diners felt like getting a towel and wiping the edges. Though there was always that interesting definable finger mark from the waiter that had disturbed the orderly pattern on the plate edge.

THE DRIZZLE ERA 1995 – 2000

Not to be outdone, the new era radical young gun chefs with their now entrenched artistic freedom (laced with marijuana) saw the potential to develop a new way of presenting food and started to drizzle plates, and again we experienced an amazing presentation revolution.

Colourful oils and sauces now were drizzled around the plate as the feature. "Must have been the marijuana". This style is still strong.

THE DIMENSION ERA 1995 – 2000

Chefs at the time realized that plate sizes did not have to change with each course, subsequently, we had the same size plate era for entrée, main and sweet, however as the entrée looked small, the main appeared large and the sweet even smaller, the outcome was a combination of the stack for the entrée, removing any sight of vegetables or starch on the main item and just serving an unaccompanied main protein became the norm, and forcing accompaniments to become an on-sell item.

Appearing on the scene was the "modernist" who delighted in presenting sweet plates with Pablo Picasso influenced features and styles using tuile paste, almond paste, chocolate twirls and other decorations to absolutely ensure that whatever was being served was totally disguised.

THE MARIJUANA LED TO THE "CLAYTON AND CONFUSION" ERA 2000 – 2005

During this era - everywhere finger food was not finger friendly. Usually a larger portion than any robust mouthful can consume in one piece, or canapés that needed a plate, or an item that was accompanied with a dipping sauce with its subsequent dribble that required a serviette.

Whatever happened to the concept that finger foods are a one-handed "petit" item to be picked and enjoyed with a glass of dry sherry in the other. For that matter what happened to the dry sherry?

Clients at cocktail functions needed three hands, one for drink, one for the canapé and one for the serviette.

And to put it all together in "2005 Gastronomy Rules" the "cold was served hot" and the "hot was served cold" with salads served on very hot plates with accompanying steaks, warm chicken skewers atop mounds of ice-cold salad.

Restaurant customers became confused and function customers angry at spoilt suits and dresses.

THE AGE OF MATURITY 2005 – 2010

The decline in fine dining and the growth of family dining in local outlets combined with a new age TV educated client who demanded fine dining standards at functions events created huge competition between the sectors.

There was a shift in family dining presenting, when food presentation styles that one would only have found in a quality restaurant a decade before was now presented with the same flair in local eateries.

Responding to the challenge, function chefs copied the standards of presentation that were normally associated with fine dining and forced fine dining to up the anti with rustic styles for example, an entrée presented in a box or a jar that replaced a plate.

food presentation - it is a question of era

At about this time we saw the introduction of a long known process of cooking food called **Sous vide** or cooking in a waterbath. This style was to be shared with an innovative scientific approach to cookery called **Molecular Gastronomy.**

THE MOLECULAR CHEF, 2010 ONWARDS

Sous vide or the slow cooking of foods in sealed bags under strict controlled temperatures that evenly cooked and concentrate flavours was not a new process, having sparsely existed for well over 40 years in the restaurant industry.

What was new was the availability of small portable inexpensive appliances required to cook in a bag. One of the benefits of sous vide cookery is cooked food looks fresh and if cooked correctly the food retains a bright natural colour. This forced chefs to focus on presenting fresh food cooked fresh as possible.

The presentation of very fresh was then augmented with highlights evolving from molecular gastronomy. Molecular Gastronomy blends physics and chemistry to transform the tastes and textures of food to create new dining experiences, using a scientific approach. Not many restaurants embraced Molecular as they did sous vide, however the unique aspects in molecular presentation caught the eye of many chefs and its style spilled out into other eateries.

We currently experience spheres, foams and sprinkling of dusts appearing on generally white plates, or very fresh cooked food using the backdrop of triangles, oblong, and hexagonal shaped plates with some dishes presented in bowls that are deeper and very wide rimmed, accentuating contrasting heights and patterns.

THE FUTURE - HOW FRESH IS FRESH ?

Natural and fresh looking is here to stay; people are diet and becoming sustainability conscious, yet still wish to push the boundaries and seek experimentation. The open plan commercial kitchen is now entrenched as a system.

Even though fine dining has diminished, there will always be a small place for sophisticated dining. People are not going to stop going out for special occasions and will still seek exotic experiences. The challenge for chefs is to continue to be highly innovative.

The demand for casual dining will grow to cater for middle income diners. The challenge for chefs will be to maintain affordability, particularly as the standard of casual dining, food preparation and presentation is now the same as was the realm of top end restaurants.

Pub food and family dining will always be popular, the challenge will be to seek and keep trained chefs to cater for a media educated public who seek restaurant standards at fast food prices.

Molecular is a fad and will be replaced by another fad, Sous vide will only be popular in fine dining and a few casual establishments.

At functions, we will see more and more "a la minute" preparation and service, for example: even canapés will not be assembled until guests arrive at the function and they will enjoy the experience of seeing their foods prepared and assembled on the spot.

AND,

Diners will wish to know more about what they are eating!

21. ettique

culinary customs
and
traditions

Adhering to culinary etiquette customs and traditions demonstrates respect for one's vocation and the unique standing as a cook or chef. Cooks and chefs share a fascinating customary code of behaviour that mirrors, or is additional to normal customary rules of polite behaviour.

These simple codes are visible signals of the level of a chef's culinary education and manners and adhering to them essential to one's professional reputation and ultimately professional success. Some rules are associated with safety, while others are simply common courtesy or tradition. The following codes are in addition to accepted social etiquette.

COOKS, CHEFS AS ROLE MODELS

Chefs, particularly sous chef and above positions, work in an environment that requires trust and teamwork.

They are in a position of responsibility that engages constantly with the brigade and expected to inspire and lead. They have set objectives, a commitment to deliver on time, adept at overcoming obstacles and demonstrate a passion for their role. Usually every member of their staff looks to them as a role model and wish one day to aspire to their status.

They are in a position to consciously and subconsciously influence, knowing that every action moulds the future of others. They are required to be and act like role models.

EMPLOYMENT

Professional cooks and chef will:

- ➤ Resign from a position properly giving reasonable notice that allows realistic time for a replacement.
- ➤ Personally inform the chef or manager before informing other kitchen staff that you are leaving.
- ➤ Follow up a verbal resignation with a briefly written letter of resignation with reasons why you are leaving.
- ➤ Leave on friendly grounds and thank their supervisors for the experience.

Professional cooks and chef do not:

- Advertise for second or third year apprentices, unless replacing a similar level of experience.
- Call in sick unless genuinely ill. Poach staff from colleagues.
- Reprimand a member of the brigade in front of others to make a point.
- Resign by email or telephone.
- Walk out from a job, no matter the reason.

IN THE KITCHEN OR AT WORK
Professional cooks and chef will:

- Address the Chef de cuisine as CHEF, unless informed that a given name may be used; while apprentice cooks and trainees should always address the Chef de cuisine as CHEF.
- Ask, "Are you able to talk" when telephoning a colleague.
- Assist someone who is "up the wall" particularly at service time.
- Say hello and goodbye to colleagues when starting or ending a shift.
- Clean up a personally made mess regardless of their position in the kitchen.
- Greet a stranger in a lift with a simple smile or hello.
- Mark a hot pot or pan on a bench to indicate danger. (Sometimes with flour)
- Step back to allow women, senior chefs or managers to enter a lift first.

Professional cooks and chef do not:

- Drink out of containers or utensils. Eat during service time or Eat or taste with their fingers.
- Telephone or visit a chef on a social call during service times. Throw food, tools or implements at anyone.

- Permit cold calling (people who arrive without an appointment) during service time.

DRESS CODES
Professional cooks and chef will:
- Dress professionally for the occasion inside or external to the kitchen.
- Wear a professional uniform in any media presentation that involves appearing or cooking in the kitchen.
- Two dress codes exist for functions for cooks and chefs. These dress codes apply when formal chefs' uniform is requested.
  - Classical: An open neck cook's jacket with a white shirt and black bow tie.

  OR
  - Modern style: A closed white cook's jacket with or without necktie.
- Both styles with black pants or slacks, black socks and black shoes. Hats and aprons are not necessary unless requested.
- Formal chefs' uniform for judges in a salon culinaire or professional cookery competition consists of a classical cook's uniform: Classical toque, white chef's jacket, necktie, black pants/ slacks, black socks and black shoes.
- Aprons are not necessary unless the judge is required to demonstrate.
- It is considered amateurish for a chef to judge in a professional cookery competition without a hat.
- Guest judges who are not chefs, visitors or photographers (in the kitchen) should be provided with a white dust coat and simple head covering.

| ettiquette - culinary customs and traditions

KNIVES AND TOOLS

Professional cooks and chef will:

- Return borrowed tools.

Professional cooks and chef do not:

- Hand or point a knife at anyone.
- Sharpen or use someone else's knife or tools without their permission.
- Throw a knife to anyone.

MEETINGS

Professional cooks and chef will:

- Apologise by email or telephone, if unable to attend a scheduled meeting.
- RSVP before required dates.
- Apologise to the host if arriving late at a meeting. Keep to prearranged appointments.
- Offer refreshments, which may be a beverage or even a simple meal to a visiting colleague.
- Shake the hand and greet colleagues at meetings, provided the meeting has not commenced.

INDUSTRY FUNCTIONS

Professional cooks and chef will:

- Send an apology if unable to attend a chef's function.
- Stop talking to others during speeches.
- On special occasions, introduce the kitchen and presiding chef to function guests.
- Turn off mobiles at meetings (unless essential or accidental one leaves the table or room during a call).

AT THE TABLE
Professional cooks and chef will:

- ➤ Turn to silent, or switch off their mobile phone.
- ➤ Remove their hat and apron.
- ➤ Wait until everyone served at the table before beginning to eat.
- ➤ Wait until the senior chef starts, before starting to eat.
- ➤ Place a knife and fork together to indicate the meal is finished.

Professional cooks and chef do not:

- ➤ Talk with your mouth full.
- ➤ Turn a glass upside down on a table.

CHEFS AS JUDGES
Professional cooks and chef will:

- ➤ Offer beverage refreshments to jury members.
- ➤ Offer more substantial food and beverage refreshments when a competition requires a commitment of more than four hours.
- ➤ Present a certificate to acknowledge the participation of a judge (Arranged by organisers and presented by the chair of the jury).
- ➤ Present a token of appreciation to competition judges. (Arranged by the organisers and presented by organisers).
- ➤ Include a signature on a competition certificate for the chief judge.
- ➤ Will not ask or expect a fee to judge a culinary competition (Except excessive transportation, accommodation or out of pocket expenses).

| ettiquette - culinary customs and traditions

GENERAL
Professional cooks and chef will:

- Be available to judge competitions or give demonstrations at local schools.
- Be willing to mentor others who inquire about the trade.

DID YOU KNOW?

- It is customary when two chefs meet, that they shake hands as a friendly gesture. More than just a greeting or an offer of congratulations, the gesture is a tradition that represents one is not holding a weapon or bearing a grudge.

  Shaking hands is a genuine salute to show the pleasure in meeting a colleague.

- If a cook or chef lays out all their knives on a torchon (tea towel or dish cloth) and systematically sharpens all of them at once in non-service time, it is a silent signal to the rest of the brigade that they have given notice to leave. Does not apply to sharpening just a few knives.

- The senior or host chef attending a chefs function should acknowledge and thank the front and back of house for the catering.

Just working like a chef is not good enough,
if you start thinking like one
you will almost certainly become one.

22. professional codes

australian culinary codes of practice

These Australian Culinary Codes of Practices were initiated by George Hill who convened a committee of working chefs in 2008 to design these codes in an act of self regulation to ensure that general professional practices of cooks/ chefs in Australia are conducted at the highest level of integrity and quality.

There are 10 codes:

1. Follow all legal and occupational regulations in my professional role and responsibilities.
2. Refrain from corrupt practices that will bring disgrace to, or damage the integrity of professional cookery.
3. Respect this culinary code of practice and encourage cooks/chefs to join one or more of the reputable commercial cook/chef organisations.
4. Be courteous to, considerate of, cooperate with colleagues and demonstrate integrity, honour and passion while accepting and celebrating my colleagues and my own achievements with dignity.
5. Seek out and mentor young persons to encourage and support them to be passionate about their vocation.
6. Share my professional knowledge and creative skills with other colleagues to advance the culinary arts.
7. Acknowledge the original source of any relevant culinary articles, food service styles, creators of fashions or unique preparations and protect the original intention of classical culinary terminology.
8. Uphold the symbol of a cook/chef uniform, particularly when I portray the image of a professional cook/chef in any public arena.
9. Endeavour to constantly improve my own knowledge and skills to professionally advance myself.
10. Strive to balance my responsibilities in work, recreation and family in harmony with each other.

23. codes definitions

australian culinary codes of practice

A **"CODE OF PRACTICE"** is, an agreed set of activities, actions, technical requirements, responsibilities or responses to events or conditions that apply to a profession, trade or industry. They are often based on international or national standards. Often these codes of practice have been agreed by a professional body in an act of self regulation and considered necessary to restrict entry into the profession and to ensure that general professional practice is conducted at the highest level of integrity and quality.

CODE 1:
Follow all legal and occupational regulations in my professional role and responsibilities.

This code of practice requires that you will follow the laws of the land and in particular comply with regulations related to your career and responsibilities. For example, you agree to follow the Occupational Health and Safety, Food Safety, Remuneration and Allowances and other local, state and federal regulations that apply to food preparation and food service.

CODE 2:
Refrain from corrupt practices that will bring disgrace to, or damage the integrity of professional cookery.

This code of practice requires you agree to be a good citizen and maintain a socially acceptable character. Including avoiding stealing, slander, fraud, vulgar language, intoxication, or drugs. Nor must you mistreat, or intentionally physically or emotionally harm, abuse, harass, stalk, threaten or otherwise violate the legal rights and privacy of others, including collecting personal information for unlawful purposes or use unethical means to gain professional advancement.

CODE 3:
Respect this culinary code of practice and encourage cooks/chefs to join one or more of the reputable commercial cook/chef organisations.

This code of practice requires you to respect the practices and objectives of other professional Cooks/Chefs organisations and encourage colleagues to join one or more of the appropriate associations.

CODE 4:
Be courteous to, considerate of, cooperate with colleagues and demonstrate integrity, honour and passion while accepting and celebrating my colleagues and my own achievements with dignity. This code of practice requires you to respect other professional

Cook's / Chef's opinions and be polite and truthful in dealing with or referring to others and admire their professional successes. This code of practice also requires you accept your own achievements with dignity.

CODE 5:
Seek out and mentor young persons to encourage and support them to be passionate about their vocation.

This code of practice requires you to encourage professional cookery training.

CODE 6:
Share my professional knowledge and creative skills with other colleagues to advance the culinary arts.

This code requires you to share your knowledge with others that will advance the culinary profession.

CODE 7:
Acknowledge the original source of any relevant culinary articles, food service styles, creators of fashions or unique preparations and protect the original intention of classical culinary terminology.

This code of practice requires you to acknowledge any substantial written or practical work originally created by another Cook/Chef. This code of practice also requires you to acknowledge and respect classical culinary terminology.

CODE 8:
Uphold the symbol of a cook/chef uniform, particularly when I portray the image of a professional cook/chef in any public arena.

This code of practices intent is to continue to intentionally brand, preserve and promote the image of a professional chef in the public arena and requires you to wear the agreed commercial cookery uniform when engaged in commercial food preparation, during professional competitions, in any cookery judging arena and on any other promotional or public occasion.

The following standards define a professional Cooks/Chefs uniform under this code:

- ➤ Preferred image that portrays a trained professional Cook or Chef and aimed to brand cooks and chefs. Recommended in any public arena, particularly in professional cookery competitions, on television or appearing in print media.

- ➤ Clean Cooks or Chefs double breasted, long sleeves, white coat with all buttons (jackets may be branded with acknowledged logos) necktie, traditional tall white toque, (white, unless otherwise formally honoured) optional white apron, black or traditional check trousers or slacks, black socks, black safe shoes. Acceptable alternatives for working conditions. Cooks or Chefs short sleeved white coat/tunic with all buttons, optional necktie, black or white cap, striped or bib white apron, socks and suitable safety shoes.

- ➤ Unacceptable image on any occasion or where public may view working Cooks or Chefs: Having no head covering in any commercial kitchen, large gimmickry patterned cloths, coloured tall toques, T shirt/ singlet, jeans, open shoes or thongs, canvas shoes or no socks.

CODE 9:
Endeavour to constantly improve my own knowledge and skills to professionally advance myself.

This code of practice requires the Cook or Chef to seek and explore challenging developing experiences and encourage others by appropriate means such as networking, further studies, entering competitions and/or innovative work experiences aimed to constantly improve themselves.

CODE 10:
Strive to balance my responsibilities in work, recreation and family in harmony with each other.

This code of practice supports a commitment to excellence and passion as a Cook/ Chef but not at the expense of one's personal life. This code of practice requires you to always consider the needs of your family and immediate loved ones in your career aspirations.

24. appendix 1

chef's
speak

Swearing and chef speak in kitchens has been around ever since the first cook existed. Swearing in a kitchen on the grounds of the hectic activity of a commercial kitchen is not an excuse. Even though the open kitchen has reduced the incidence of openly swearing, particularly as chefs realise they cannot use expletives in front of clients, unfortunately it still is a commonplace occurrence in closed kitchens.

Every kitchen becomes acutely stressful at some time, more often during service time when the demands and pressures of heat and emotional stress come together to form a physical and emotional electrifying environment.

There are numerous expletives used in kitchens not identified here. However, working in a commercial kitchen will be a learning curve for some.

Swearing is mainly a way of releasing steam, anger, frustration, or anguish generally used by cooks and chefs who are unable to handle a situation and express their anguish in other ways. Swearing can be a means of signalling solidarity in a pressurised kitchen, while "*chefs speak*" are a part of the natural humour of a chef that is used between the brigade staff to express their thoughts and feelings.

The following is a list of the more common chefs speak:
(with apologies for the use of unavoidable expressions)

Aggro	*Someone who is in a bad mood.*
Away	*("Take away") Call to send a table of covers to the dining room.*
Bad news	*Trouble maker in the kitchen.*
Behind you	*Warnings when carrying something hot. Alternative: Hot.*
Cowboy	*Member of staff who lacks the ability to do their job. (Not gender specific).*
Canned	*A person is intoxicated or drunk.*
Colonial Goose	*Colloquialism for mutton.*

appendix 1 - chef's speak

Cheap as chips	Alternative for French-fries.
Check the plate	Tells cooks in an open kitchen that an attractive guest has arrived.
Crumpet	A desirable female. The male equivalent is Hunk.
Dragon	The name applied to an overbearing female member of staff.
Eff off	To tell someone to "Go forth and multiply"
Far out	Implies the best or excellent.
Funny Farm	Highly disorganised day season or kitchen.
Get knotted	See "Eff off".
Gravy train	Easy.
In the weeds	Unable to cope. A similar expression to being up the wall.
It is swimming	Already frying in the fryer.
In the hole	In the oven.
Junket	Informs that a cook is on a break.
Kill it	Cook well done.
Knackered	Tired worn out.
Loose screw	Considered insane or a loner in a kitchen.
Nifty	Whatever it is its COOL.
No Show	In the kitchen - Staff member who has not arrived for work.
No Show	In the dining room - A table booking that has not arrived.
Ok	Shouted response at service. Individuals have their own unique response.
Off	Indicates an item is not available on the menu.
Outboard	Indicates an immersion blender.
Pass	The hot press or race where plates are kept hot and ready to go.
On - plus	Mise- en -place is completely ready.
Prep	Same as Mise- en - place or preparation before service.

Race	Hot press point where orders are dispensed in the kitchen.
Rubber	A tea towel or torchon the dishcloth usually folded on the hip.
Rubber	Latex finger stool resembling a condom
Screwed	One did not get the shift they were after.
Silly season	A time of the year when the kitchen is at its busiest.
Spice it	More season is required.
Take away	Call to collect a table of orders (Often "Away").
Tied - up	Someone in the kitchen is unavailable.
Up the wall	In desperate need for assistance. (The opposite meaning of On-plus).
VIP	Literally very important person.
Whiz	Blend in a food processor.
Wannabe	See Cowboy.
Waste it	Throw away.
X	Indicates 'mixed' when written on a docket as in xgrill or xsalad.
Yes chef	The first and only words you really need to know in any kitchen.

25. appendix 2

common culinary technical terms and cookery descriptions

Specialised vocabularies evolve in a trade or profession so that everyone who works in that industry, knows, understands and uses the terms to standardise industry practices and protect their profession.

Culinary terminology and commercial cookery descriptions represent a commonly agreed way that cooks and chefs will apply a method, cut a shape, follow a recipe, garnish a dish, name a product, present a dish, use a technique, identify a title, and more.

Culinary terminology is shorthand communication in a kitchen. It facilitates leaving one job and quickly assimilating into another and as importantly, correct usage of culinary terms especially on menus educates the public.

Originally derived from French technical recipe books, many technical terms and cookery descriptions are now a global chef's language. A cook or chef will have a substantial repertoire of terms, some of which follow. Many other terms exist especially in kitchens that focus on one culture. An Indian restaurant will have its own set as will Italian, Japanese, Mexican, and others.

The following list is representative of common Western culinary terminology. There are literally thousands of culinary terms that assist cooks and chefs with their mobility from kitchen to kitchen, country to country and used to build bridges across cultures.

This following list is not a reference; it is a sample listing and demonstrates a reason why there is a need for culinary terminology. The list is indicative of a typical cook or chef's understanding of their language.

| appendix 2 - common culinary technical terms & cookery descriptions

A SAMPLE OF CULINARY TERMS THAT DESCRIBE FOUNDATION PREPARATIONS.

A cook or chef will be able to interpret and apply these terms in a commercial environment.

Aioli	A cold egg and oil emulsion with olive oil and garlic.
Ballontine	Boned stuffed leg of poultry or game bird.
Beurre blanc	Emulsified sauce from wine or vinegar, butter and cream.
Bouquet garni	Bunch of fresh herbs parsley, thyme, bay leaf, and celery.
Concassé	Blanched, skinned, de-seeded and chopped tomatoes.
Confit	Meat or poultry cooked and preserved in its own fat.
Crème Anglaise	English custard, fresh custard made with eggs and milk.
Pesto	Paste with basil, garlic, oil, coriander, nuts and parmesan.
Pilaf	Braised rice.
Soufflé	A very light sweet or savoury dish; served hot or cold.

Additionally a competent cook will know:

Béarnaise, Béchamel, Beurre manié, Blanquette, Canapé, Chantilly Cream, Compote, Consommé, Coulis, Court bouillon, Crème pâtissière, Crêpes, Croûte, Croûtons, Demi glace, Duxelles, Eggwash, Espagnole, Farce, Fleuron, Flûte, Fumet, Galantine, Genoese, Gâteau, Glace de Viande, Mesclun, Mousseline, Panada, Pâté, Paupiette, Praline, Profiterole, Rissole, Roux, Sabayon, Soubise, Tartare, Tournedos, Tuilles, Vacherin, Velouté, Vinaigrette, and Zabaglione.

A SAMPLE OF CULINARY TERMS THAT DESCRIBE CULINARY TECHNIQUES AND PROCESSES

A cook will be able to interpret and apply these terms in a commercial environment.

Bard	Cover game and poultry with a strip of pork fat.
Blind bake	Pre cook pastry.
Cook out	Fully cooking the flour in a roux or dish.
Correct	To adjust the seasoning, consistency or colour of a dish.
Crumb	To coat in breadcrumbs.
Deglaze	Swill out a pan with wine, stock or water.
Garni	Abbreviation for garnish, or to decorate with a food.
Gratinate	To brown under the salamander.
Knead	Work dough by pressing and folding it with hands.
Marinate	To soak meat in a liquid to impart flavour.
Reduce	To concentrate a liquid by simmering.
Season	Adjust the flavour with salt, pepper, herbs and spices.

Additionally a competent cook will know:

Clouté, Cordon, En cocotte, En Papillote, Flambé, Glaze, Infuse, Lard, Macerate, Mask, Pique, Proof, Prove and Sauté.

| appendix 2 - common culinary technical terms & cookery descriptions

A SAMPLE OF CULINARY TERMS THAT DESCRIBE PRODUCTS, INGREDIENTS AND EQUIPTMENTS

A cook will be able to interpret and apply these terms in a commercial environment.

Agar-agar	Gelatine substance made from seaweed.
Basmati	Long-grained rice
Boudin	A white sausage of veal, pork, and chicken.
Carpaccio	Thin slices of raw red meat, also applied to fish.
Chinois	A conical strainer.
Chipolata	Thin small pork sausage.
Couscous	A pasta from semolina (Durum wheat flour).
Crème fraîche	A light sour cream.
Mandolin	Manual vegetable slicer.
Pancetta	Cured pork belly that is rolled and tied.
Terrine	An earthenware dish used for making pâtés.

Additionally a competent cook will know:
Angle hair, Arroz, Aspic, Bain-marie, Bouchée, Caul, Clarification, Cocotte, Coupe, Dariole, Friture, Kugelhopf, Nori, Nougat, Orzo, Pak choi, Pappardelle, Parisienne scoop, Ramekin, Tandoor and Timbale.

A SAMPLE OF CULINARY TERMS THAT DESCRIBE GARNISHES, FLAVOURS AND MENU DESCRIPTIONS

A cook will be able to interpret and apply these terms in a commercial environment.

à la	In the style of.
à la carte menu	An individual priced menu.
Antipasto	Italian appetiser.
Au gratin	Sprinkled with cheese or breadcrumbs and browned.
Mezze	Middle Eastern appetiser or a spread of appetisers.
Ragout	Stew.
Risotto	An Italian rice dish made with stock and butter.
Smorgasbord	Swedish buffet of many dishes.
Sorbet	Water ice, served as a refresher between courses.
Table d'hôte	A menu with a set price.
Torte	German for cake or flan.
Vol-au-Vent	Round puff pastry cases.

Additionally a competent cook will know:
à la française, à la minute, à l'anglaise, Amandine, Andalouse, Brochette, Cover, Diablé, Dubarry, Entrée, Florentine, Forestière, Haute, Hors d'oeuvre, Lyonnaise, Normande, Piéce de résistance, Poussin, Rijsttafel and Tagine.

appendix 2 - common culinary technical terms & cookery descriptions

A SAMPLE OF CULINARY TERMS THAT DESCRIBE POPULAR INTERNATIONAL CUISINE

A competent cook would be familiar with and can use their technical skills and a standard recipe to prepare commercial quantities of:

Bruschetta	Toast brushed with olive oil and fresh garlic and topping.
Carbonnade	Beef braised in beer.
Gazpacho	A cold soup from fresh tomatoes and cucumber.
Gnocchi	Small Italian dumplings cooked in boiling water.
Minestrone	An Italian vegetable soup with beans and pasta or rice.
Navarin	Lamb or mutton stew with onions and potatoes.
Osso Bucco	Veal shank braised with vegetables, aromatics, and stock.
Panna cotta	Cooked-cream Italian dessert similar to Bavarois.
Saltimbocca	Pan fried slices of veal, rolled ham, sage and cheese.

Additionally a competent cook will know:

Baba, Baba Ganoush, Baked Alaska, Beignets, Biryani, Bisque, Borscht, Bouillabaisse, Brioche, Bubble and squeak, Caesar salad, Cannelloni, Calzone, Carbonara, Char siu, Cock-a-Leekie, Cordon Bleu, Coulibiac, Croquembouche, Crudités, Fricassée, Frittata, Gazpacho, Goulash, Guacamole, Gumbo, Jambalaya, Kedgeree, Matelote, Moussaka, Mulligatawny, Nasi Goreng, Navarin, Paella, Pakorha, Petits fours, Ratatouille, Salmis, Samosa, Sashimi, Tabbouleh, Tapenade, Taramasalata, Tempura, Teriyaki, Vichyssoise, Vindaloo and Zakouski.

A SAMPLE OF CULINARY TERMS THAT DESCRIBE CUTS AND SHAPES

A cook will be able to interpret and apply these terms in a commercial environment.

Brunoise	Small dice of fruit or vegetables.
Chiffonade	A very fine julienne of green leaf vegetables.
Croquette	Cylindrical shaped foods, crumbed and fried.
Darne (Cutlet)	A slice of round fish on the bone otherwise named a cutlet.
Escalope	Small thin slice of meat, usually chicken or veal.
Goujonettes	As in goujons but thinner and smaller.
Jardinière	Vegetables cut into batons.
Julienne	Vegetables cut into fine strips.
Macédoine	Fruit or vegetables cut into dice.
Medallion	Small round cut of meat.
Mirepoix	Roughly chopped onion, carrot, and celery.

Additionally a competent cook will know:
Agnolotti, Aiguillette, Alumette, Delice, Gaufrette, Noisette, Penne, Quenelle, Rosette, Roulade and Tronçon.

| appendix 2 - common culinary technical terms & cookery descriptions

A SAMPLE OF CULINARY TERMS THAT DESCRIBE TITLES AND SYSTEMS

A competent cook would be familiar with and know their meaning:

Brigade	The collective term for the kitchen staff.
Apprentice cook	Indentured apprentice.
Chef de cuisine	Head chef of a kitchen.
Chef	Chef de partie
Commis	Assistant cook.
Cook	Commercial cook.
Executive Chef	Senior chef manager with two or more kitchens.
Food Service Assistant	Simple food preparer and cleaner.
Garde manger	Cold larder cook
Pâtissier	Pastry cook.
Sous Chef	Second in command or deputy Chef de cuisine.
Trainee cooks	Persons in training.

Additional titles and descriptions associated with specialists in the classical hierarchy system, seldom found in modern kitchens, nevertheless known by a competent cook.

Brigade system (Kitchen hierarchy established by Auguste Escoffier). Aboyeur, Chef de nuit, Entremétière, Grillardin, Legumier, Plongeur, Poissonnier, Potager, Rôtisseur, Saucier and Tournant.

26. hot off the press

penalty rates, are they an industry problem or a political issue?

The current penalty rates debate focuses on the wrong issue' for decades, the industry has debated the problem' not the root cause. It is not about penalty rates. The underlying issue is about appropriate level of compensation to hire a professionally trained person.

Obviously, and rightly, business owners like to reduce costs, and employees strive to maximize their salary. However, there are three fundamentals;

1. Unless a business makes profit, no one wins,
2. Unless a professionally skilled person supports a business, no one wins,
3. Last, and the most influential, unless people in a career are adequately compensated for their skills, fundamentals 1 and 2 will not work.

A career in hospitality is 24/7, even more fundamental, an occupation that requires "one to work when others are at play", that is an undeniable fact and accepted by normal intelligent people who work in, or about to join the hospitality industry.

Let's cut to the chase, it is irrational to suggest that one is worth more on a Monday because it's a public holiday than any other normal Monday. It is just as illogical to suggest penalty rates should be cut, because we cannot afford to pay more for staff on the Monday of a public holiday.

What we should be debating is the overall annual remuneration for a job that needs a professionally trained person who is on duty on the public holiday or any other day or night.

There is unfortunately a community mindset, including industry leaders that believe the hospitality industry (especially back of house) does not require academically minded or reasonably intelligent people. Therefore, they can be classed as "low paid workers".

Therein lies a paradox, an occupation that requires a worker to be physically fit, mentally adept, intelligent, skilled, have professional

| hot off the press

perspective, flexible, and is experienced, does not equate to a low paid worker, nor with that industrial attitude, will the industry be able to attract appropriate people.

Currently, industry professionals are appropriately compensated for their skills by a "top up" with penalty rates, so tread carefully with this decision; either remove penalty rates and at the same time substantially increase salary potential, or remove penalty rates without any compensation and exacerbate the shortage of skilled workers to the detriment of everyone's business and the whole industry.

That is the bottom line.

Industry leaders need to stop playing politics and realise that they need to compensate with a salary that befits a professional, demand, and recruit people with sufficient skills and academic ability, return to employing cooks and not ill-prepared pseudonym chefs or untrained part-time waiters in situations that warrant a professional, and return to proper in-house training.

Then, and only then, will the industry stimulate the environment to attract people with the ability to be professional in their workplace, and intelligent enough to realise that their occupation requires a 24/7 mindset.

Moreover, everyone will win, because professional staff working for professional managers will bring back clients.

27. hot off the press

contradictions;

are they

showing a

dying profession?

At the very beginning of this book, we illustrated many inaccurate descriptions in the commercial cookery industry derived from an unrestrained cookery industry.

Therefore, it is fitting to close by illustrating examples where misguided attitudes and the unrestrained industry have developed blatant contradictions and untruths in Australian food culture.

- How is it possible that the Australian restaurant industry is widely promoted to be excellent and among the best in the world; when the average restaurant score in food guides across Australia in hundreds of restaurant evaluations is 13/20. Who would be happy if their children averaged 65% in a final year test?

- Why do the public believe restaurant reviews will always reflect the quality of a restaurant experience?

- How can restaurant reviewers assess a restaurant purely on their experience of a single meal without ever considering attitudes, consistency, reliability, dress standards, hygiene, commercial success, and more?

- How is it possible to be the "The best restaurant" "The chef" "The best recipe"

- Why do many people believe pictures of food in magazines or on menus come straight from the pot to the plate, without extreme sprucing?

- How is it that chefs cited with "A Chefs Hat", are not willing to wear one as a symbolic image of their vocation and award?

- How is it that many of the very people who call for the abolition of penalty rates do not work on weekends?

- How is it possible to be an apprentice chef, when chef is a position of responsibility, whilst an apprentice is learning to cook and graduates with a "cookery" qualification?

- How can one be a "qualified chef" when a chef describes a person's authority and a cook identifies their expertise?

hot off the press - contradictions

- *How is possible that chefs believe they are professionals, yet many attend functions looking like rag dolls with un-ironed clothes and dirty shoes, while supposedly being trained in grooming and hygiene.*

- *Why are the majority of great chefs not good at marketing themselves, but very skilled at cooking, while many celebrity chefs show they are not good at cooking but very skilled at marketing.*

- *Why do people who believe a chefs job is only a practical one, and does not require a well-educated person, not aware the chefs cost menus, write memos, and need to understand legislation.*

- *Why do the media believe that every chef is an "Executive chef" without questioning their real role experience and responsibility?*

- *How is it that one can be "The Chef of the year", when only assessed on one day in clinical competition conditions?*

- *Why do we have light meals on menus offering deep fried fish and chips?*

- *How many chefs who strongly support sustainability, do not check to see if the seafood they buy is on the endangered list?*

- *How can one sell a "chicken sausage schnitzel"?*

- *How can one advertise a chicken strudel that is chicken made with puff pastry?*

George always brings reality, excitement and challenge to the table. He is unafraid to speak what many think and acts always

to protect the professional standing of the proponents of commercial cookery. George has always had a visionary approach and this book confirms that he remains at the cutting edge in the culinary arts. Let's not return to the "Good old days" but use this book to make tomorrow memorable.

Norma Seip, 2014

ADDENDUM

I started this book explaining where I began to develop my philosophy, and conclude with my current opinion.

At twenty-seven years old, I discovered that I not only needed the skills, attitude, knowledge and experience to be a cook, but the backdrop of a good general education to be a senior chef. I found it necessary to return to evening classes and weekend studies for many years, while still working full-time and at the expense of quality time in the normally limited family time available to a chef.

I discovered that only the silly leave school at fifteen, thinking that being a chef is merely a practical discipline. No one advised me at fifteen, that to progress up the career ladder a senior chef needs to know how to write memos, attend management meetings, discuss functions with clients, negotiate with vendors, calculate menu prices, manage budgets in cost centres, and being a chef is more than just putting food on a plate.

Cooks now want to become a chef immediately without having gone through the trial by fire and time. An attitude aided by a general public mindset who believe that one does not need an initial sound education to be a successful senior chef.

One need to realise, it depends upon the level of responsibility and fame one wish to achieve, how quick one chooses to get there, and a personal decision of taking the hard or the easy pathway to success.

GEORGE HILL
President of the Australian Institute of Technical Chefs

The Institute of Technical Chefs:

- Is an association of chefs with strict professional entry and requirements.
- Aims to identify and register commercial professional cooks who have the necessary experience, qualifications, fitness and commitment.
- An association of chefs who focus on standards in commercial cookery.

AM I CHEF ? © George E. Hill 2014

http://salonculinaire.com
http://auschef.com
http://chefpedia.org
http://www.technicalchef.com/
Wikipedia.org George Hill (Chef)

www.ingramcontent.com/pod-product-compliance
Lightning Source LLC
Chambersburg PA
CBHW071921290426
44110CB00013B/1434